6990

B109.

Also by NORMAN HARPER

First Daily

Spik o the Place

Stronach Vol I

Stronach Vol II

Stronach Vol III

The Stronach Tapes

A Dash o Doric
(with Robbie Shepherd)

Anither Dash o Doric
(with Robbie Shepherd)

Weeks in the Howe

Norman Harper

Aberdeen Journals Ltd

First published in 1999 by
ABERDEEN JOURNALS LTD
Mastrick, Aberdeen, Scotland AB15 6DF

10 9 8 7 6 5 4 3 2 1

Cover design by Susan Bell

www.press-and-journal.co.uk

British Library Cataloguing-in-publication data
A catalogue record for this volume
is available on request

ISBN 1 901300 06 4

Printed in Scotland by Polestar AUP Aberdeen Ltd.

Dedicated to the senior journalists of the Press and Journal
of the late 1970s — particularly Ron Knox and Ethel Simpson
— who rolled up their sleeves to try planing a few of the
rougher edges off the new boy. Work still in progress.

Contents

Foreword

by Derek Tucker
Editor
The Press and Journal

ONE of the greatest misconceptions held by the general public is that journalists can write. They can't. Or, at least, most of us can't. Yes, we can report on what we see and what we hear, but writing what we FEEL is a totally different skill, beyond the grasp of most of us. Note that I include myself in that.

To be able to write is to be able to translate one's thoughts or, more usually, everyone else's thoughts, on the events we encounter in everyday life and present them as though they were being spoken directly to the reader. To be able to write humorously is a gift limited to the very fortunate few.

When Norman Harper reminded me that I had agreed to write the foreword for his latest book, my first thought was that he had taken advantage of my notoriously bad memory. My second was that, once again, I had opened my mouth without engaging my brain.

It is, nevertheless, an honour to be asked to introduce a writer who, through more years than he would care to remember, has been travelling the length and breadth of Scotland observing the idiosyncrasies of folk and storing them in his brain, neatly filed for ready retrieval at the appropriate time.

It is Norman's powers of observation, coupled with his unique writing style which have made him a firm favourite in households from Shetland to Stirling and from Stonehaven to Stornoway.

Which of us, in all honesty, has never consulted Oxford or Chambers to find if the word describing this week in the howe really exists?

Who has not thought *quite right* when he has pricked the ego of another so-called expert trying to tell us how we should live our lives?

And who has not enjoyed the easy style with which he has demolished the latest pearl of wisdom to emanate from Westminster or, more recently, Holyrood?

To those of you who answered: "Not me" to any of the above, I ask only that you reconsider the question when you have read — and enjoyed — this compilation of Norman's work.

Derek Tucker
October, 1999

Introduction

by Norman Harper

I N THE great roll of human vanity, one of the greatest must be to assume that your thoughts, opinions, memories and feelings are worth sharing with others — especially twice a week in a newspaper column. The only greater vanity is compiling those thoughts, opinions, memories and feelings into book form so that people may read them all over again.

I am innocent on both counts. Becoming a columnist was not my idea. Neither was it my idea to publish this book. I deferred to far greater powers. I'll explain later.

My first think-piece, as we call them in the trade, appeared in The Press and Journal in the summer of 1978. I was still a trainee journalist, doing a three-month stint in the Features Department, which all young journalists did in those days to give them a flavour of life beyond the newsroom.

Instantly, I liked the challenge of constructing the words differently. We had to write just as tightly and clearly as any news reporter, but we had to cope with a far broader and emptier canvas. It was so rewarding that I began writing other pieces at home in my spare time, just to see if I could handle various styles and subjects.

Genuinely, I cannot remember how what followed happened, but one of those pieces found its way into my top drawer at work and languished there for about a fortnight. It might have been there yet had not the Features Editor at the time, Ron Knox, wanted to leave me a confidential document while I was away on some assignment or other and decided to leave it in my drawer. After I had returned, he waited until the rest of the Features staff had gone home and asked about the item he had spotted accidentally.

I can remember clearly saying: "Och, I was plucking up the courage to let you see it." Equally clearly, I can remember him saying: "Pluck up the courage? Did you think I would fling you out of the window or something? It goes into the paper on Thursday."

Roll forward nine years now. By 1987, I was Features Editor myself and the newspaper was going through a major redesign to keep it looking fresh and ahead of the competition.

One of the pitches made as a Features Department contribution to this grand revamp was to redesign the Weekend Journal Saturday supplement and to have its front page anchored by four columnists, each contributing once a month and each with different styles, voices and bees in their bonnets.

We signed up Jim Naughtie, son of Rothiemay and later anchor of BBC classical music and Radio 4; Dr Jim Hunter, one-time features writer on the Press and Journal staff, and much later chairman of Highlands and Islands Enterprise, and Bill Howatson, our then Farming Editor. We had still not secured the services of our fourth even when the new beast was launch on August 1.

It was not for the want of trying. We had approached more than a dozen likely candidates, some of whom did not want to commit themselves to regular writing; some who felt they were not up to it, and some who submitted samples which weren't quite what we were looking for.

So I wrote the fourth column in that debut month, intending it as a stopgap until we found someone proper. Someone proper never came, and I contributed to Week Ending, as we called the slot, for the next six years. Some of those pieces appear in this compilation. You'll spot them easily enough: they're the ones that *don't* begin with: "It has been a xxxxx week in the howe."

And that brings us to the spring of 1993, by which time our then new Editor, Derek Tucker, had been in post for six months. By that time, he had developed a feel for his newspaper and had gone to a great deal of trouble to speak to readers from all walks of life, and everywhere from Shetland to Central Region and the Western Isles to Buchan, before making a series of key changes.

He told me he was killing Week Ending. I confess it was something of a relief, because producing a monthly column from scratch is a bit of a tyrant. I might even have told him as much.

"Instead," he said, "I'm having daily columnists, Monday to Saturday, and I want you to do Wednesdays."

I don't recall what I thought. Or, if I do, it's safer not to say here.

"And Saturdays, as well."

He was quite specific in his brief, too. The Wednesday column was to be strictly a review of some quirky incident that had happened to me in the previous seven days. When I ventured that that might not be exactly compelling reading, he said that I might want to use any such experience as a springboard to explore a wider subject, but he would prefer that I developed a personal relationship with the readers.

The Saturday column, by contrast, had to start each week by being resolutely tough; pricking pomposity and exploring the hypocrisy and idiocy of a news issue of the week. It would be followed by developing and commenting on three or four odd news items that readers might have missed.

In the space of five minutes, 13 columns a year had become 92.

So now you understand why my claim at the start of this Introduction — that I never sought to become a columnist — was perfectly true. It was always thrust upon me.

That is much the same excuse for this book. I had no notion of producing any such compilation but, truthfully, readers had begun asking for it, which is flattering, and my North-east upbringing means I am not quite sure how to cope with the implied compliment. Anyway, if we know anything about readers of The Press and Journal, it's that they expect to get what they want.

To maintain my modesty and keep myself out of at least some of the flak which attends all public writing, I have also managed to steer clear of the third, and greatest, vanity: deciding which columns were the best and, thus, worth including here.

I have left that to a small selection committee, headed by my wife, Alison, and composed of several other family members and

11

friends; all readers of the Press and Journal, and all with differing tastes. If you wonder at any point: "Why on earth is that in here?", they are the ones you'll need to ask. They read through 1,000 columns before fixing on these 52; devotion I don't deserve.

Finally, a few words of thanks. Not once in 20 years has anyone at the Press and Journal told me that I am not permitted to write on a particular subject, or instructed me to take a potshot at something. Nor has anyone asked me to change or soften my views to suit the paper's image or commercial prospects. A free hand like that is rare, indeed, and I'm grateful for the privilege.

Even when I have expressed views that are held honestly, but which have angered the people they were calculated to anger, and those people, on occasion, have made veiled threats to the Editor or the MD, I have been given only encouragement to keep it up. Usually, the people who get angriest with newspapers either have very thin skins, take themselves and their sacred cows too seriously, or would prefer that something was kept out of the public gaze altogether. That makes them wonderful targets.

Second, I must thank the readers. Like all columnists, I get letters. Some are angry, some snide, and I believe I also get some anonymous letters (which I am never given, so their authors could save the price of a stamp). The nasty ones are few, however, and lose me no sleep.

On the whole, the mailbag is a joy, and the response gratifying, even when someone is chiding me gently. Reading the feedback is the highlight of my afternoon, and has sparked more columns than the correspondents in question could possibly guess. Indeed, the Saturday column has evolved in such a way that I could barely function without the eagle eyes and ears of legions of readers from all points throughout the Press and Journal circulation area.

Anyway, you'll be wanting to get on with your book. Here come 52 examples culled from 12 years, beginning in August, 1987. They're in no particular order. Just dip in.

And I hope you enjoy yourself.

Norman Harper
The Howe
October, 1999

The
Columns

1. SCHOOL MEALS and BAD LANGUAGE

Or why toad-in-the-hole will never beat macaroni

━━━ ━━━ ━━━ ━━━

"By the time the food was distributed to the tinies at the bottom end, it amounted to very little. Up at the top end, the heaps were wondrous to behold."

SCHOOL macaroni. Who doesn't have fond memories of it? Thick with a floury sauce and half-melted grated cheddar, and a bubbling, leathery skin so laden with cheese bree that when you bit into it your eyes and mouth watered at the same time.

With beetroot and two or three roast tatties, it never failed to kittle up even the least athletic pupil for a blustery, grey afternoon on the games field.

I have been fortunate enough to dine in many parts of the world, in some of the most celebrated hotels, since my primary-school days, but no one has yet come up with a dish which beats school macaroni for warmth, comfort and satisfaction. So don't criticise the school-meals service to me. I have always thought that dinner-ladies got a bad Press unjustly, for I loved school meals.

While half the children were playing football in the playground at morning break, and the other half were belting the living daylights out of each other, I would be hovering around the door to the kitchens, looking forward to lunchtime and savouring the humid, wafting aromas of watery potatoes, banana custard, haggis and jam sponge.

Our canteen was an old wartime stone-and-lime hut. It held

about 25 tables of eight, with 50 hard wooden benches, seating four to a bench. These tables and benches were ranked down both sides, with one row up the middle.

My primary school had a four-year secondary attached, and we shared canteen facilities. This brought about a hierarchical system at lunchtimes. The big boys and girls sat in the four places to left of each oblong table. The primary schoolchildren sat in the four to the right.

The meal monitor — the biggest boy or girl — was responsible for collecting a tray from the kitchen of all the paraphernalia the octet needed. His or her opposite number was responsible for dishing up.

This was not entirely an equable system. Distribution by consumer is always a dangerous practice. By the time the food was distributed to the tinies at the bottom end, it amounted to very little. Up at the top end, the heaps were wondrous to behold.

One brave little chap complained about the paltry nutrition before him, I remember, and a big boy leaned across and studied the minuscule plateful.

"Quite right," said the monitor, after expansive discussion with others at his end of the table. "That's a disgrace." He then removed half a sausage and two tatties. "That's far too much for a little sharger like you."

Indirectly, dinner ladies have been responsible for a few heart-stopping moments. A colleague remembers the day his eight-year-old came home and, at the tea table, announced: "I had sex today."

The boy's mother choked, while father, burning with curiosity but trying to appear nonchalant, said: "Oh? In the school?"

"Yes," said the boy, quite unabashed. "It was great."

"Sex?" said father.

"Yes. Really good. I'll maybe have it again tomorrow if I have the time."

"I see. And where does this happen?"

The boy looked at his dad as if his dad was thoroughly dense. "In the canteen." Then he continued: "I've never had it before, but most of the boys do it, so I tried it and I liked it."

"Sex," said father.

"Yes," said the boy, getting a little irritated. "Sex." Then, seeing his father's bewilderment, he added wearily: "Sex! *Secs!* Second helpings!"

Second helpings were my undoing, I must confess. At my primary school, the second-helpings system operated by having the dinner-ladies on the prowl round the hall, with huge dishes of unconsumed comestibles. They stopped only if someone put up a hand.

Occasionally, there appeared a particular dinner-lady who bore a permanently dejected look on her face. Nothing, but nothing, would persuade this woman to look anything other than utterly miserable.

It seemed to me, being a very compassionate eight-year-old, that she got very little trade for her doughballs or her dollops of sago, and I decided that that was probably what was disappointing her.

"What a sad lady," I always thought, studying her. So, every time she shuffled past the end of my table, bucket of custard, stew or mashed tatties hanging in the crook of her arm, I felt overwhelmed with pity. I would put up my hand whether I liked the stuff or not, and a dollop would be whacked out in front of me; a dollop which conscience forced me to eat. A lesson I learned very young: compassion is good for the soul, but bad for your insides.

However, the school-meals incident which I remember above all others concerns the enterprising nature of whoever planned the menus. It must have been about 1965, for I would have been about eight. Anxious to break out of the daily round of macaroni, mince, fish or stew, in a rash moment the canteen decided to produce Toad in the Hole.

That day, when the meal monitors at the head of each bench lifted the covers gingerly off each container, the blank stares told all of us that something was amiss. Each monitor dished up with pronounced apathy. This was the one time the tinies found their plates heaped to the ceiling.

We soldiered bravely, but it was one of the canteen's few abject failures. And that was when one of the big boys, in a stage

WEEKS in the HOWE

whisper, announced several tables away: "Toad in the Hole? This tastes like the xxxxxxx hole!"

Gales of laughter swept round the canteen. To an eight-year-old, the expletive meant nothing. I had never heard the word before. But the big boys' and girls' laughter was infectious. I was soon roaring with the hysteria of it all, although I hadn't a clue why.

That night at home, we were having our tea in customarily silent and solemn mood. I was trying desperately to remember the funny incident at that day's lunch, but I couldn't work out what it was.

My mother noticed the perplexed look on my face. "Stop playing with your food," she said. "What's wrong?"

Suddenly, the lunchtime phrase came to me. "This tastes like a xxxxxxx hole!" I blurted, and sat back, beaming, waiting for the gales of laughter I had heard at lunchtime.

Yea, verily, mighty was the anger of Mrs Harper. In her tempest she didst smite her begotten son, Norman, about the lugs and didst heat his behind mightily and send him to his bed with no repast and, yea, with tears in his eyes.

And thoughts of a delicious and comforting plate of school macaroni didst dance in his head until, all alone, he cried himself to sleep.

For three weeks after this column appeared in early 1990, I received invitations to various school canteens to try their macaroni.

Never reluctant to scoff a school meal, I accepted many and very nearly became sick of the stuff. But not quite.

I'm happy to report that the traditional dish is alive and well and sustaining a new generation.

2. STARSKY AND HUTCH (and Norman)

Or why to refuse to go on police night patrol in Chicago

▬ ▬ ▬ ▬

*"I'm not ashamed to say I was sweating. I was frightened.
I had good reason to be frightened. And that made it all
the more frightening."*

The ageing blue-and-white Chevrolet Caprice slowed outside a five-storey apartment block. It was dark. It was humid. Sounds of a wild party were coming from the second floor.

Officer Jim Maloney wasn't interested in the party. Instead, he trained the car's roof searchlight on to a top-floor flat. The windows had been smashed; the frames were charred, and the brickwork was blackened on all sides. "Bad fire last night," he said. "Guy had to knot sheets together to get out."

I peered out and up. "A lucky escape," I said, still gawping.

"Nope," said Maloney, switching off the light. "Knots came apart. Broke his neck. Helluva mess on the sidewalk. Should've been a better boy scout."

Maloney has been with his Chicago precinct for 10 years. "You have to remember, death's an everyday thing to us," he said. He paused for a moment. "Maybe you have to excuse us. It's our way of coping. We see a whole lot of sickening stuff."

"What about the Rodney King verdict?" I said. [*Weeks before this column appeared in May, 1992, four LA policemen had been acquitted of assaulting a black man, despite clear video evidence. That led directly to the infamous LA riots.*]

Maloney looked at his partner and buddy, Driver Patrolman Don Rose. It was Rose who spoke eventually. "Tell you what," he said quietly. "I don't know a guy in this precinct, even this whole city, who wasn't expecting the book to be thrown at those guys.

"Did you see the video in Scotland? Jeez, man, those guys set back policing in this country twenty years. Maybe thirty. They've made our jobs tougher than ever. Every cop in this country's livin on a knife-edge. A guy's kind of scared to do his job right, know what I mean? Every time you go for an arrest, you think: 'Is this guy gonna screw me for police brutality, or what?' You can't do a good police job thinking like that. Things happen too fast."

He trailed off as he slowed to eye a gang of black youths slouching against a wall on a street corner. There was a pointed exchange of stares, but nothing more. We drove on.

Maloney and Rose are both in their mid-30s. They joined police academy on the same day, fulfilling a lifelong ambition together. They say they are only slightly more disillusioned now, not because of the LA riots, but because of the vast scale of crime in the US and their sense of the futility of the individual officer.

"You get a glow when you nail a guy," said Maloney, "but you have to take so much crap from politicians and the media and the public. It's real depressin. You nail a crime and you're someone's friend."

"Till the next time the someone gets a traffic ticket," added Rose, and they both managed a thin laugh.

By now we were approaching Cabrini Green, a 1960s high-rise experiment in public housing, where the residents, all black or Latino, and 95% unemployed, while away the hours shooting each other. It was just past midnight.

"Sometimes they shoot at us," said Maloney. I wasn't sure if I was having my leg pulled or if I should believe him. They looked at each other, then grinned.

"Nah, you're safe enough, Norm," said Rose. "Don't scare the guy, Maloney. You know it's at least a week since a cop got shot up here. Say, Norm, did you sign the form back at the precinct?"

"Yes," I said. "I signed a disclaimer."

"Great," said Maloney, satisfied. "If anything happens, the

captain can say he didn't know anything about you and it's nothing to do with us."

Ahead of us, little knots of distinctly unsavoury types scowled at us as the patrol car cruised past slowly. I retreated as far down into the seat as possible. The smaller the target the better, I decided.

A moped shot out of an alley, ridden by a black youth at least 10 sizes too big for it. "That bike got Wisconsin plates, Don?" asked Maloney, sitting up. He pulled a printout from behind the sun visor and scanned it. "Something on the job list about a bike on Wisconsin plates stolen last night," said Maloney, still scanning.

At that, the youth threw the bike down in the middle of the street and began running for an alley.

Rose floored the gas. The car shot off. I was thrown back.

We screeched up the alley, missing bins and fire escapes by not more than inches.

I waited for a pile of empty cardboard boxes seen in all the best cop shows, but suddenly Rose screeched to a halt.

The youth had run up another alley too narrow for the car.

Rose and Maloney dashed out and disappeared up the alley in hot pursuit.

I have to say this was all most exciting. The surge of adrenalin was indescribable. I was living an episode of Starsky and Hutch.

And that was roughly the point when I realised I was sitting alone in a police car, with both doors open, in the middle of Chicago's most notorious black slum 10 days after the LA riots.

And suddenly it all seemed quiet.

Too quiet.

I couldn't decide if I should pretend that I wasn't there, or if I should make myself obvious and hope somebody mistook me for a cop. Preferably a cop with a big gun. A lot of guns. And a truncheon. I'm not ashamed to say I was sweating. I was frightened. I had good reason to be frightened. And that made it all the more frightening.

Then the back door flew open. I stifled a little involuntary yelp.

"Scoot over," barked Maloney. Obediently, I slid across the rear bench. He stuffed in beside me the biggest black 19-year-old you have ever seen, whose hands were cuffed behind his back. "We got his buddy," explained Maloney, "but we gotta catch Evel Knievel still. Doncha go away now." He slammed the door shut.

I stared straight ahead. Then I tried to wrap myself into as small a parcel as possible, still staring straight ahead. Beside me, 20 stones of suspect, panting, shook his head, moaning: "Shit, man. Ah din' do nuthin. I's jes standin there. I din' do nuthin."

From the corner of my eye, I caught him raising his head slowly to study me. I snapped to look out of my side of the car, as if admiring the view on a Sunday-afternoon drive up Deeside.

"What *you* done, man?" he said.

"Oh," I said, in a frightfully British accent. "Actually, I haven't done anything."

"Dey b'lieve you?"

At that, Maloney and Rose were back. "Missed him," said Maloney, out of breath. "Clear over a ten-foot fence."

He lifted the radio transceiver on his shoulder. "Twenty-four, twenty-three. Bringing in a suspect about the Wisconsin moped. Can you send the wagon to pick it up?

"And can you have a cuppa coffee ready for our ride-along from Scotland?

"He looks like he's havin a rough night."

━━ ━━ ━━ ━━

All I wanted to do while I was on patrol was talking about the dangers of Chicago policing, but Maloney and Rose kept turning the conversation round to golf. Every Scot had to be a golfing expert, they believed (erroneously).

Both were keen golfers and were adamant that I had to fix them free passes for the Old Course at St Andrews. I failed miserably.

3. REMEMBERING MY GRANDMOTHER

Or why not to assume that children don't grieve

___ ___ ___ ___

*"I was oblivious to her trauma, not just because I was
only seven but because, through her illness, she showed me
no other face than the smile I had always known."*

THIRTY years ago today, my grandmother died. It was a slow death, even as cancer deaths go. Confined to bed at home for many months, she suffered great pain. The longer she lay, the thinner and more frail she became until, on August 30, 1965, she passed away.

I was seven years old.

I can't claim any sophisticated memory of what happened that summer; mine is the perspective of a seven-year-old who knew only that his grandmother was desperately ill and that he didn't much care for it.

So I would sit quietly in my grandparents' house, on the landing by the stained-glass window and the big Chinese urn, and watch as the district nurse in her vivid-blue uniform climbed the stair past me, with a gentle smile, and disappeared into the front-left bedroom. On other days, either of the two village doctors would arrive.

Fifteen or twenty minutes later, the door would open and there would be cheery farewells, followed immediately by hushed conversations as my mother or grandfather or aunts led the nurse or doctor down to the front room for more-detailed discussion.

Not party to adult affairs, I would sit on the landing and look up to the closed door and wonder. Sometimes I crept up to it, stopped for a moment or two, listening hard, then grasped the wooden knob, opened the door and stood there, looking.

To the best of my recollection, she seemed small and lost in a huge bed. To a seven year old, she didn't look ill. She had no bandages. There was no blood. She was just tired. Incredibly tired.

But she grew increasingly tired, until the day when someone — I forget who — felt it was better that I didn't go into the room on my own, for she was too exhausted to deal with me. I didn't see her again.

Thirty years on, I realise I was oblivious to virtually all her trauma, not just because I was only seven but because, throughout her illness, she showed me no other face than the smile I had always known.

I missed her then and I miss her now.

On the day she died, I had been back to school for just a week. The first I knew that something was awry was about 200 yards from our house, as I walked home that Monday afternoon.

Kicking stones along the gutter, I looked up and saw in the distance our neighbour standing in her front garden. There was nothing unusual in that; our neighbour kept a bonnie garden and was working on it on many afternoons when I arrived home from school.

That afternoon was different. That afternoon, she was standing looking for me.

As I drew closer and made for our own gate, she called to me over the fence and told me that my mother had had to go away in a hurry and that my four-year-old brother and I would be staying with them for the night.

Late that evening, long after my brother and I were in bed, I heard my mother's voice in the living-room. A few moments later, the door opened and there she stood, asking us to get up.

In our pyjamas, we settled by the fire and she presented my brother and me with two toy cars. I can remember them still: maroon and white Ford Corsairs, and how strange it felt to be given toys at such an odd hour for no good reason.

The following morning, as I appeared for breakfast, the

neighbour took me to one side, sat me down and said just a single sentence as gently as she could:

"Your grandma's sleeping."

I was only seven, but I didn't misunderstand, not even for a moment. I knew exactly what the euphemism meant and I began howling.

For some weeks, I harboured the unspoken hope that perhaps the neighbour had made a mistake; that sleeping really did mean sleeping and that my grandmother would soon be restored to us and in fine health. It was a hope that evaporated agonisingly slowly.

Seven or eight years ago, a villager who had known my grandmother very well asked if I remembered her. I thought it an odd question then and find it peculiar now.

I remember my grandmother with exceptional clarity; almost as if she had not died. Not a week passes but I don't think of her.

I can see her making bannocks.

I can remember the taste of her custard.

I remember her washing the pudding bowls with flying pheasants round the edges.

I remember being chastised gently for eating so much gulshach.

I remember her cardigans, her slippers.

And later, when the illness had taken hold, I remember watching my mother cut up fruit pastilles and hiding pills inside before offering my grandmother "a sweetie".

What would she have been like had she lived? That, I cannot answer, although I have wondered often.

What would she have been like as a 90-year-old? What would a reserved and gentle lady have made of the 1990s?

What would she have made of me?

Adults who imagine that small people survive the death of a grandparent almost intact, by dint of tender years, are mistaken. The death of a loved one is traumatic at any age, and its effects prolonged.

It is especially hard on children; for people who have not fully had a chance to know a person before death can only wonder, or learn second-hand.

That is the cruelty of death as it affects children. Seven years was not long enough. As every year passes, it seems pitifully shorter and shorter. My only tangible reminders of her are two photographs. They are among my most treasured possessions.

Today, looking back, I can console myself with two thoughts: although seven years is short, it is still several years more than many of us are given together.

And what she meant in those seven years has coloured the subsequent 30 only for the good.

She made, and makes, all the difference.

▬▬ ▬▬ ▬▬ ▬▬

This was one of the most difficult columns to write, for obvious reasons, but it is probably the one that I'm most glad I did, and I'm pleased that the selection team decided to include it.

Baring your soul like that is not easy, particularly for a man, and particularly to northern Scotland. I had not done it before and I have not done it again.

I was gratified, however, that it had such a positive response when it appeared in August, 1995, including one letter from a woman in Moray, I think it was, who said she was cutting it out and keeping it in a drawer by her bedside so that whenever she wanted "a good cry", she could take it out and re-read it.

Best of all were the letters from some of my grandmother's contemporaries who were able to fill in some blanks for me and compounded my impression of someone I knew too little.

4. THE SCIENCE OF LUGGING-IN

Or why you daren't laugh at overheard conversations

■■■   ■■■   ■■■   ■■■

*"Bella was large, with a plastic shopping bag hanging in
the crook of her arm. Violet looked as if a puff of wind
would blow her into the slush at the side of the street."*

I HAVE a confession to make. I eavesdrop. In queues, waiting-
rooms, trains, theatres, I love listening to other people's
conversations. They say this is a healthy sign in a writer, but
it conflicts with my upbringing, which tells me that such
behaviour is rude and intrusive.

I try not to, but other people's words and phrases drift across
and set me thinking. Some playwrights call them triggers; others
call them hooks. They are phrases which contain so much drama
that an audience is compelled to pay attention.

Consider a few examples.

". . . it's his poor wife I feel sorry for . . ."

". . . and then his phone bill came in and it was £920 . . ."

". . . and the doctor said he hadn't seen a case like it in all his
forty years in medicine . . ."

Any one of these almost compels you to lug in and find out
more. One of my colleagues became so engrossed in a
conversation between two women in the seat in front of him on
the bus that he held on deliberately for three stops past his own
so he could hear the end of the story. It cost him a soaking in the
rain as he walked back, but it was well worth it, he felt.

I remember standing in a queue in the checkout at a shop in my home village a few years ago when a pensioner ahead of me reached the till. She was puffing and blowing and grimacing as if in great pain. She gripped the small of her back.

"My goodness, Mrs ******," said the assistant. "You're looking in terrible pain. What's worst with you? Have you been to the doctor?" She carried on ringing up items on the till.

"There's nae doctor can help me, lass," said Mrs ******. She leaned forward conspiratorially, and about half the queue did the same, me included.

"It's the change o life," she whispered.

She leaned back and the whole of the rest of the queue snapped back and began staring at their feet or into mid-space as if they hadn't heard a thing.

"Aye," she said a little more loudly. "There's nae question. I've got the mennapods."

A few Christmases ago, an aunt of mine was travelling on a bus from Aberdeen to Culter. A five-year-old boy was standing on one of the seats, swaying beside his mother and singing, almost shouting, tunelessly at the top of his voice, over and over again: "Oh, Little Town of Bethlehem." Not the whole hymn, just the first line. Over and over again.

The first dozen times were tuneless enough, but it began to drill right through every other passenger. Over and over again: "Oh, Little Town of Bethlehem."

So, eventually, a woman leaned forward and, very sweetly, said: "My, what a good little singer you are. Now, tell me, do you know Once in Royal David's City?"

The little lad stared at her for a few moments, thought deeply, then nodded and announced: "Aye. A lotta rubbish."

And, louder and more tunelessly than ever: "Oh, Little Town of Bethlehem.

But the best current story about eavesdropping was told to me only two nights ago. I have to confess that this time I was not the eavesdropper, but I was told it by an impeccable source.

The tale's beauty is that it depicts North-east conversation at its natural best. It is expressive without being fulsome, empathetic without being cloying and is riddled with acute observation.

It concerns the unfortunate demise of a small dog under the wheels of a bus. My source did not witness the incident, but she was standing in a bus queue in a North-east town a few days later.

Ahead of her were two pensioners. One, and we'll call her Bella, was a large, amply upholstered woman, with a plastic shopping bag hanging in the crook of her arm.

The companion, and we'll call her Violet, was a small woman, as tiny as Bella was plump, who looked as if a puff of wind would blow her into the slush at the side of the street. The contrast was visually humorous, but it was the conversation that caught my friend's attention.

Before animal-lovers write to berate me for being so despicable as to find humour in the suffering of one of God's innocent creatures, I should point out that I put food out for the birds in winter. I swerve in cars when rabbits run out in front of me. I stop and lift hedgehogs off roads. I do not make fun of animals. I love animals. I love them.

The humour in this anecdote lies not in the suffering of the animal. The humour lies in the dead-pan, sanguine reaction of the two pensioners. They are not to be berated, either, for they are of good North-east stock and were expressing their sorrow in a naturally subdued and effacing North-east way. They would be horrified and upset to be accused of finding fun.

This is the humour of observation, and it works because it is subconsciously so black as to be worthy of Chekhov. It proves that ordinary folk make a far better job of dialogue than any scriptwriter.

". . . and the bus driver said he couldna stop," said Bella.

"Couldna stop," agreed Violet.

"The little lassie wis terrible upset," said Bella. "Terrible upset. Racked wi sobs. It wis her doggie, efter aa. There wis nae consolin her."

"Nae consolin," agreed Violet.

"The doggie jist ran oot," said Bella.

"Jist ran oot," said Violet. "Jist ran oot."

"The bus driver?" said Bella. "Fite as a sheet. *Fite - as - a - sheet.* That man wisna weel. I tell ye, he looked mair upset nor the little lassie. He wis near greetin himsel. And the bobby, he jist stood there takkin notes."

"Takkin notes," said Violet.

"The driver couldna stop, ye see," said Bella. He telt the bobby that if he'd stopped, folk stannin inside the bus micht hiv been hurtit. So he'd nae option."

"Nae option," agreed Violet.

"Bit he wis terrible sorry," said Bella.

"Terrible sorry," agreed Violet.

They paused as if considering the angst and trauma suffered by the bus driver and the little girl, united in their grief. Then:

"It wis a bonnie little thing as weel," said Bella sadly. "A bonnie little doggie."

"A bonnie little doggie," agreed Violet.

Then they stared mournfully at the slush for a few moments while considering the demise of the unfortunate canine.

At that, the bus hove in sight and Bella peered at her handful of small change. She drew a deep sigh as if to signify that life goes on.

"Weel," she said cheerily. "A bonnie little doggie it micht hiv been, bit it's flat as a kipper noo."

One or two animal-lovers got in touch to say that they hadn't been offended at all. Indeed, one included a tale that was far more graphic and which I couldn't use in print but, again, it dealt with the deadpan reaction of elderly people, rather than the suffering of a pet.

A couple of people asked where the bus stop in question was. It was in West High Street, Inverurie.

5. DUTY AT THE CHALK FACE

Or why the toughest audience is nine years old

▬▬ ▬▬ ▬▬ ▬▬

*"They can also be dogged inquisitors. One class became
engrossed in the question of libel — a pretty advanced
topic for a primary school."*

JOURNALISM is seasonal. As in any other profession, there
are peaks and troughs of activity and satisfaction, allied
closely to the passing months.

While July and August fairly amble by in news terms, October
and November whizz past so fiercely we barely have time to
loosen our grips on our pens. And now a new journalism season
is with us; one which my colleagues in TV and radio confirm is a
Topsy that has growed and growed and growed.

The school-talks season creeps up on us from the middle of May
and lasts for roughly six weeks. It's no coincidence that this is the
time when teachers are casting around for something to fill the
post O-Grade limbo.

There are ways of approaching a potential speaker. You stand a
better chance of success if you do not, as one woman did, call and
announce: "Mr Harper, I have a gap in my fourth-year timetable
on May 22 at 3pm and I'd like you to fill it."

Neither do you let slip a couple of sentences into a call that "the
man from the environmental health was coming to talk about dirty
kitchens, but he can't manage and we thought of you".

A very pleasant country teacher would have slighted someone
huffier than I had she asked him, as she asked me: "Now, do you

have a video or a film or slides or something? I don't know if having you talking for the whole time is going to keep their attention."

Experience has taught me that I always ask to meet the teacher at the front door of the school. While still a novice, I used to visit the school office, as security and courtesy demanded, and then amble through labyrinthine corridors looking for room numbers. It was complicated enough in itself, without the raggier elements of the second-year girls giggling and the jannie prowling after me at a discreet distance in case I molested anyone.

So now teachers run the gauntlet with me. Occasionally, this causes even more of a stir, especially in schools where pupils are not shy of voicing their curiosity. We pass knots of teenagers playing cards in the cloakrooms, then (whisper, whisper, whisper) a shout: "Miss! Is 'at the new Bible mannie?"

"No, Graham, it's not!" And we carry on in full sail. Then comes a mutter from the cloakroom: "Well, he looks like a Bible mannie tae me." It all conspires to chip away at your stage confidence and you haven't even reached the classroom.

The preamble in the classroom is fascinating to an outsider. Teachers, I have concluded, deserve every penny of their salaries and more, for supervising 35 high-spirited young adults must be very wearing.

At a careers-week talk in one new Aberdeen secondary school, the careers teacher organised a headcount and came up with 36.

"Thirty-six!" she said. "Thirty-six? I've only thirty-five names on my clipboard. Who's here who shouldn't be here?"

Silence.

"Come on! Out with it or Mr Harper's leaving right this minute." I sat up straight and took my hands out of my pockets. If I'd had chewing-gum, it would have been stuck under the desk double-quick.

Presently, a little hand went up and trembled at the back. "Yes, Sharon, what are you doing hovering around where you shouldn't be hovering?"

"Please, miss, I really wintit travel and tourism, bit I've gotten putten in here instead."

These minor hiccups aside, the talks themselves usually go fairly briskly once I get into my stride. Primary schools are my favourites, for Primary Six and Seven pupils get over their shyness in five minutes flat and I can build up a rapport very quickly.

On my first primary sortie, I asked the teacher: "They won't be nervous, will they?" and she looked at me quizically. Within two minutes of starting, I could she what she had meant, for they got tore in.

"What's the most bloodiest accident you've seen?" "What's the biggest crash you've seen?" "Have you ever been really sick?"

"What's your most embarrassing moment?" and I always tell them about the time, as a very junior reporter, when I was sitting in the front row at the dress rehearsal of an Aberdeen school's panto, turned to a man next to me and said: "I don't know where they dragged up the female lead, but they shouldn't have bothered."

He said: "I'm the depute rector, and that's my daughter."

Primary schools are also the places not to be caught off your guard. One sweet-faced 10-year-old at a country school asked: "Div ye ken the Editor?" I said I did.

"Div ye hae arguments with the Editor?" I thought for a moment. "We have discussions," I said.

"Div ye like the Editor?" And the teacher cut in. "My goodness, Lisa, you're asking an awful lot of questions about the Editor."

"Yes," said Lisa. "My dad kens the Editor."

And another narrow squeak passed into history.

They can also be dogged inquisitors. One class became engrossed in the question of libel — a pretty advanced topic for a primary school. "Is it true that the Editor gets put in jail if there's a mistake in the paper?" asked one lad.

"Well," I said, "it's true that the buck stops with an editor usually. If there was a really big mistake, he would be the one summoned to court and, yes, maybe even sent to jail."

A gleeful look crossed his face. "Ooh," he said. "That would be good, eh?" Wisely, I kept my counsel.

We moved on to safer ground. I began trying to explain the difference between tabloid and broadsheet newspapers — a difficult enough concept for adults, or even some of the professionals within the industry, to grasp. Eventually, I asked them which size of paper they preferred. "Broadsheet," said one. "Broadsheet," said another. "Broadsheet," said a third.

I was mystified. It ran against all the received wisdom from customer surveys and industry projections, which held that tabloids appealed at the younger end of the market, and broadsheets at the older. "Why broadsheet?" I asked.

"Because you always get better value for money with the Press and Journal. There's a lot more in it."

How could I not warm to a class like that? Although it sounded suspiciously as if someone had a relative in senior management at the Lang Stracht, so I made a mental note to be careful.

By my favourite school-talk story came from Turriff Academy, after I had talked to their first-years. I was escorted back to the staffroom by one teacher, while another stayed to settle the class. When she returned, I asked how she thought it had gone. Had they been interested? Was I too advanced or was it too simplistic?

"I asked them all that," she said.

"And what did they say?"

"Kerry said the best bit was your tie."

▬▬ ▬▬ ▬▬ ▬▬

> *I don't do talks of any description now, to children or to adults, although I was on the speaking circuit for seven long years from the late 1980s. They take more time to prepare than people think, and it's impossible to do them justice, keep the commitments and cope with the vagaries of a journalist's schedule at the same time.*
>
> *But it was good fun while it lasted. Even Kerry.*

6. DEALING SCHOOLS AN UNFAIR HAND

Or why league tables are a waste of time and money

■■ ■■ ■■ ■■

"You might as well say that everyone who opens an aspirin bottle is half-way to being a doctor. Or everyone who writes to a newspaper could make it as a journalist."

PERHAPS you saw the recent Press and Journal front page which listed schools throughout the North and North-east and gave the Government-released exam results for each. First, you looked for the results of your old school, or the school your children attend. Next, you looked for neighbouring schools and compared them. Next you looked for for other schools with which your family might have connections and compared those. Last, you scanned the complete list, looking for the top performers and the duffers.

That's what I did myself. So did most of my colleagues. So did most of my friends. So did most teachers. It was the natural thing to do.

We were wrong to do it.

You might as well compare the yield of an acre of grain in the Saskatchewan prairies with the yield of an acre in Armenia. You can't judge these farmers' comparative successes because you're not comparing like with like.

In Saskatchewan, agricultural scientists, botanists, geneticists, meteorologists, politicians, commerce and clients are all pulling with the farmer in the same direction, all working hard. Small wonder that the yield is high virtually every time. When a problem occurs, it can be dealt with promptly and efficiently. In Armenia, farmers have temperamental pre-war equipment and seed suppliers often unabashed about the quality of their grain. There is a sense of futility of the individual against great odds. When a problem occurs, there are so many other problems being juggled that it must simply take its turn. The wonder is that Armenia produces any grain at all.

The Saskatchewan and Armenian farmers might be equally hard-working, yet the same level of hard work in Saskatchewan produces more spectacular results than exactly the same hard work in Armenia. The hand of circumstance generally waves kindly at the Saskatchewan farmer and smacks the Armenian in the teeth. There's the difference.

The same is true of schools and the exam-results tables. With apologies and respect to Banchory or Lerwick, high "scores" don't mean that Banchory Academy or Anderson High are filled to the rafters with star teachers.

Neither do they mean that staff at Wick High, Invergordon Academy, or Torry or Northfield Academies in Aberdeen, are shiftless, incompetent and scraped from the dregs at the bottom of the pedagogical barrel.

Exam statistics don't show good teaching and bad teaching. They show schools where everyone is pulling in the right direction: schools which have hit the right mix of dozens of different criteria: good curriculum, adequate funding, committed staff, social advantage and — the key — involved parents who produce enthusiastic pupils.

No one can engineer that mix. Most of these factors lie outwith a school's control and teachers must make the best of the hand they are dealt.

Few teachers, no matter how brilliant and dedicated, will turn a dull or rebellious pupil into a candidate for the groves of academe if that pupil's parents are apathetic or unable to provide support and encouragement at home, or if the pupil's peer group exerts immense pressure to rebel.

Parents, pupils and social set are just as important in a teaching equation.

Part of teaching's trouble is that all of us have been to school and too many of us suppose that that makes us experts on education. You might as well say that everyone who opens an aspirin bottle is half-way to being a doctor, or everyone who writes a letter to a newspaper could make it as a journalist.

The debate should not harangue teachers or regimes at low-result schools. The debate should concentrate on how to encourage more parents to become more active and interested in their children's education, and to see it as a partnership with the school.

A school in which teachers know that their burdens and concerns and aims are shared actively by most parents is a fortunate school, indeed. That's when exam results (if these are an effective yardstick at all) become impressive.

It is easy to judge the success of most things. With a newspaper, you examine its circulation (that is why you have made the Press and Journal one of the top three regional mornings in the UK).

You can't do that with teaching. Columns of sales figures don't work for a profession in which most of the work and travails are unseen.

How do you draw up statistics which account for the hours spent coping with a single difficult pupil and for trying to limit the damage he causes to his peer group?

How do you account for days and weeks chivvying and encouraging a single struggler; for keeping abreast of the latest educational fad when all you want is breathing space to adjust to the last one; for dealing with irate parents who refuse to believe that their angel is a devil the minute he sets foot across the school gates, and for parents who imagine that their only function is to feed, clothe and house a child and leave the upbringing to teachers?

One teacher I meet during each year's Press and Journal schools debating competition told me ruefully that last summer she had bumped into the mother of a notorious third-year hooligan. She was regaled with stories of misdeeds and vandalism the boy had been up to.

The catalogue was given quite freely and with no shame, and

then the mother said: "I jist telt him: 'Wait till you're back at the school. They'll sort ye oot.' " That just about sums it up. Too many parents expecting too much.

Certainly, there are poor teachers in low-scoring schools. This column doesn't excuse them.

There are brilliant teachers in high-scoring schools. I don't suggest that their results happen without hard work.

But there are many first-rate teachers doing their damnedest in low-result schools, and it ill behoves politicians and public (most of whom wouldn't know their three Rs from their elbow) to fix on statistics and use them as a stick.

Teachers don't need me to defend them; they're more capable of that on their own account. It must be sorely trying, though, to have politicians and public puff and blow in such a facile and destructive way without considering deeper principles and tackling those.

By and large, teachers do the best they can with diminished funding, diminished prestige, diminished morale, minimal support — and precious few thanks.

A little humble and objective contemplation by all those eager and ready critics might not go amiss.

I still believe firmly that league tables — be they for schools, hospitals or any public service — are thoroughly pointless. Nothing in life is that black and white.

Many people assumed that Mrs Harper, a teacher, had a hand in this column. I promise that she didn't, although, as you would understand, it hit the spot with many beleaguered teachers.

7. ROUND AND ROUND A RAGGED ROCK

Or why to worry when old school friends get in touch years later

"The acceleration pushed my stomach away down into my legs. The sensation and G-Force are far, far more pronounced than on the most despicable rollercoaster."

IT WAS a voice from the past. Alan Shand, an old primary-school friend, called to say he had been reading the Press and Journal motoring page for several months. "I've been reading the car tests," he said, "but how would you like to do some real travelling? How about if I take you round the Knockhill circuit as a passenger in a motorbike and sidecar?"

A quaint image of 1950s AA men wafted into mind; tucked up and cosy from the elements, bedecked in flying scarf and goggles, equipped with a flask of coffee and sandwiches.

Rather fancying myself in the romance of flying scarf and full-length leather coat, I said: "Delighted."

I travelled down to the circuit on the Sunday morning, singing along to the tape in the car and admiring sunny Fife. Two miles from the circuit , I fancied I heard engines screaming rather loudly for sidecars and I turned down the radio-cassette a notch or two, but I persuaded myself it was a synthesiser or some such on the tape.

When I parked at the circuit carpark; climbed the steps into the control room, and met the formidable Mrs Binkie Chapman, secretary for the Knockhill meetings, I was decidedly more on edge.

The sidecars were certainly making a lot more noise than AA sidecars used to.

Then she ushered me through to the viewing gallery. The "sidecars" turned out to be little more than tea-trays welded to the sides of motorbikes, and they were belting round the circuit at more than 100mph.

Prostrate passengers stayed on board by dint of two tiny metal handles, gripping for their very lives, while tarmac flashed past at sound-barrier speeds less than one inch beneath the ends of their noses.

Mrs Chapman ushered me out of her way and into the cold, pointing vaguely southwards. "You'll find Alan somewhere over at the back there," she said. "By the way, I come from Aberdeen originally."

I can't remember if I congratulated her or not, but I stumbled around the back lot for several minutes, pushing, dazed, through crowds of motorbike groupies, mechanics, speed-stained riders and those poor, poor "passengers" hirpling past, clutching crochlie ankles, necks, wrists, elbows and knees and moaning softly.

Then I spotted my host.

"Thanks for coming," he said. "We spun off in that last heat. Going backwards for a while. Fair speed. Neil [the usual passenger] just hung on in there, though. He's good at that. I've only lost him twice."

Alan ushered me along to where his crew, most of them FPs of Alford Primary School, was tending the bike. It was like walking into a reunion.

I borrowed a full set of body leathers, boots, gloves and helmet and managed a quick change, whimpering softly, in the back of a Transit van. By the time I emerged, Alan was fired up and ready to head down for a test spin on the track while everyone else was at lunch.

"I'll take it easy on you,' he shouted over the screaming engine. "Lean to the left into the left-handers and right into the rights. Keep your knees together. Lie as flat as possible and grip.

"Grip that top handle with your left hand and the side one with your right. If you get worried or nervy or anything, it's not a problem; just tap me on the shoulder."

I gave him a wan thumbs-up, but it wasn't until we were bouncing out on to the track that I realised that if I did let go to tap him on the shoulder, I would shoot off the back quicker than a turkey escaping from Bernard Matthews.

I was about to tap him on the shoulder and say: "Excuse me," but I . . ." when he lined up on the grid and knocked the breath from me instantly as he turned on the juice.

I will admit to a little involuntary yelp as the sheer acceleration pushed my stomach away down into my legs. The sensation and G-Force are far, far more pronounced than on even the most despicable rollercoaster.

Mercifully, my gasps, gulps and pants steamed up the visor. I couldn't see a blooming thing, which was just as well. The bends were not so bad, but the anticipation of emerging on to a straight and knowing that Alan was about to shoot up six gears in quick succession, building from 30mph to more than 100 in the space of a few yards, was more than flesh could bear. I managed a silent thank-you for not having had breakfast.

On the second lap, the long straight down in front of the grandstand and hundreds of bemused spectators was mildly pleasant, even although I had just tightened my grip on the grab handles and was staring into the tray floor.

By the third lap, I was beginning to enjoy myself. I had become accustomed to the pounding acceleration which seemed to stretch me to 7ft and the crippling deceleration which squashed me to less than four.

I had managed to banish the thought that half an inch from my toes was tarmac at 100m.p.h., and I was managing to lean into the corners as instructed. Horrendous speed and sheer vulnerability had actually become quite intoxicating.

But your arm strength lasts for only so long when you're unaccustomed to riding sidecar. As we approached the end of the third lap, I found myself listening and longing for a drop in the engine note, signalling that we were heading for the pits.

If that note had risen,   heralding a fourth lap,   I doubt that my grip would have lasted. Thankfully, Alan had decided that I had probably had enough. We rumbled to a halt next to the crew. "How was that?" asked Alan, removing his helmet.

"A lot better than I thought," I said. "I can see why people get a taste for it. Have you got a bucket?"

"We're off to Belgium shortly," he said. "We'll be at the TT in the Isle of Man, as well."

"It must be quite expensive," I said, pulling off my gauntlets. I tried forlornly to grip my pen and notebook, but my hands refused to work, still locked in a life-or-death grip. With a script that was even more of a hen's crawl than usual, I gave up and committed the conversation to memory.

Alan used to race solo bikes, but got a taste for sidecars two years ago and has raced Formula Two with his partner, Neil Miller, of Kintore, since then. "It *is* expensive," he said. "Shirlaw's help a lot with sponsorship and we're always keen to find more.

"But I'm pleased you enjoyed it. It's good fun, isn't it? Neil's a good passenger. A good passenger gets to the stage that he can go round the track at full speed hardly hanging on at all."

"Have you ever ridden as a passenger? I asked.

"Are you joking?" said Alan. "Do I look daft?"

Alan gave up bikes a few years after this column appeared in 1989. When I received another call in 1995, he was telling me that his new hobby was flying microlite aircraft. Would I like to try?

Call me daft, call me easily led, but I went along and tried that, too. It was much safer than it looks but, take it from me, you wouldn't believe how freezing cold it is at 400ft on even the hottest day.

8. MOSCOW, WE HAVE A PROBLEM

Or how to pay good money to scare yourself rigid

*"An extra frisson attends proceedings when you are the
only soul among 150 hysterical Russians who doesn't
know why you should be hysterical."*

THERE'S not another airline quite like Aeroflot. At least, I
hope there isn't. Every horror story you hear about Russia's
national carrier is true. Aeroflot is proof absolute that big is
very rarely beautiful. The first leg of my recent flight home from
Murmansk to Moscow should have been one of those simple little
two-hour hops that any Western airline takes in its stride.

But this was Aeroflot, the airline which, at a rough estimate, has
had more fatal mischanters than any other. The airline which the
Foreign Office has advised Britons to avoid if at all possible. The
airline which the Civil Aviation Authority wanted to ban from
British airspace because of its safety and maintenance standards.

And the airline on which I was booked to fly from Moscow to
Murmansk and back. Someone at the Lang Stracht is trying to tell
me something.

This pilgrim's travails begin with the homeward journey, striding
out over the Murmansk Airport tarmac in the 6am darkness.

It was -12C and there had been an overnight snowfall of Arctic
proportions. Most airlines would prepare for flight by clarting their
aircraft with de-icing fluid and carrying out doubly stringent pre-
flight checks. Aeroflot has a little man in overalls walking up and
down the wings brushing off snow with a roadsweeper's broom.

43

I climbed the steps and looked for my seat. The interior fitments of our Tupolev 154 were from the sub-Oxfam school of interior design. The carpets had teased ragged at the joins and bare metal shone below. The seat material, a cheery green-and-yellow stripe, bore the stains of years of spilled food and drink, or evidence of a multitude of previous personal traumas that had attended the hairier moments of Russian aviation.

So I sat into my seat by the window — and found myself staring at the cabin ceiling. The mechanism to keep the seatback upright was broken. Since a two-hour flight prostrate held little appeal, I sneaked into the middle seat of the row of three, intending to plead ignorance when its bona-fide occupant turned up.

When my travelling companion arrived, he was a Mongolian businessman with a persistent phlegm problem. He stood in the aisle, studying his ticket, and I steeled myself for howls of outrage. Instead, he simply shrugged his shoulders and squeezed past my knees into the faulty seat.

He, too, flopped back but, clearly a seasoned Aeroflot client, decided this was a bonus, fell asleep and began snoring.

The travelling companion to my right arrived. Miss Irkutsk Tractor Parts 1973, a matron of considerable magnitude, was wearing a full-length imitation-vinyl coat and, judging by her perfume, had just finished her shift at Murmansk Fish Processors.

Others began arriving, carrying TVs, video-recorders and heated trolleys. When the stewardess explained that these large objects could not be piled in the aisles for safety reasons, the passengers became animated and aggressive and she retreated. Half the consumer durables of the Kola Peninsula stayed where they were.

So let us take stock.

There I am, in a plane fit only for the scrapyard, belonging to an airline which, only days before, had crashed a state-of-the-art Airbus A320 in Siberia, killing all on board, because its captain allowed his children to take the controls.

I am jammed between a snoring Mongolian and a monumental fishwife. I am unable to speak Russian and I know that, if there is an emergency, video-recorders will take precedence over me.

The takeoff went well. The climb was fine. We levelled out and set course for Moscow. Two hours stuck between a snoring Mongolian and a fishwife seems longer than two hours, strangely enough. When I looked at my watch, I understood why; we had been flying for almost two and a half hours.

Moments later, the public-address system hummed and the captain spoke in Russian. The effect was dramatic. At once, all around me, there was agitation. Colour was draining from faces. Sleepers were being prodded awake. People were sitting upright, jabbering in near-hysterics, looking for a stewardess.

An air emergency — for I presumed that that was what it was — is bad enough when you understand what is going on, but an extra frisson attends proceedings when you are the only soul among 150 hysterical Russians who doesn't know why you should be hysterical.

I watched the stewardess explaining the problem to other passengers. From her hand movements, I deduced that the undercarriage had stuck.

The Mongolian began shouting and I felt like smacking him in the mouth. The fishwife was staring straight ahead as if several thousand volts were passing through her underwear. Children were crying. Mostly, people were staring at the stewardess, a slip of a lassie who seemed as nervous as everyone else, desperate for reassurance. Curious things go through your mind at moments like these. First, you remember all the newsreel footage of smoking, mangled metal after other airline crashes.

Then you hear the funereal tones of Michael Buerk: "It is believed one Briton was on board. Positive identification will follow once they collect all his bits from three Moscow suburbs."

Then you tell yourself that aviation is the safest form of travel, and you feel better. Until you remember that you're flying on Aeroflot. Finally, you bless your Editor, that fine fellow, that prince among journalists, for sending you on the assignment.

We banked sharply and began a slow descent to what turned out to be an alternative, emergency airfield, 80 miles to the opposite side of Moscow. There was a reassuring clunk from under the fuselage which, as seasoned travellers will know, is a sign that the undercarriage is at least down, if not locked.

Things in the cabin became eerily silent as the runway hove in sight and we continued gliding towards it. The cabin lights dimmed and people stared at their knees in the brace position. Everything became strangely peaceful.

The last thing you hear on a landing is the power being cut to the engines seconds before the aircraft settles on to the runway. Those few seconds seemed like weeks.

And finally the plane landed.

Bang! Clunk! Rumble-rumble-rumble!

We were intact. No crash. In one piece.

Most passengers cheered and clapped as the plane taxied to a somewhat random parking spot on the apron. The stewardess began her customary spiel, presumably: "Welcome to Moscow. The time is 9.34. The temperature is -6C and I have wet my pants."

Air has rarely smelled so sweet as when I climbed out on to the steps and headed for the terminal.

And the British Airways livery has never looked so good as when, later that day, I climbed the steps of the flight to London, knowing I was in far safer hands. I could have kissed that plane.

Indeed, there is most certainly not another airline quite like Aeroflot. For that, may the Lord make us truly thankful.

Far worse than the trauma of that trip was the knowledge that I had been offered the choice of flying SAS and Braathens up through Norway and still chose the Aeroflot experience "just to see".

But what I grudged most was the $100 taxi fare (dollars only, no roubles) to get from one side of Moscow to the British Airways flight at the other. Aeroflot never replied to my reimbursement claim.

9. WW, MAN OF LAUGHTER

Or why it's important to remember the good ones

▬ ▬ ▬ ▬

*"A dedicated community fund-raiser, a most considerate
and thoughtful colleague and, above all, the best story-
teller and natural comedian I had the privilege to meet."*

TODAY, I want to talk about one of my good friends. He
was known throughout Scottish journalism and British
industry. He was on first-name terms with virtually
everyone in his home town, yet moved with equal ease in the
most exalted national company. He had a stern and incontro-
vertible belief in a journalist's responsibility to his readers, yet he
was blessed with one of the most effervescent senses of humour I
have known.

His name was Willie Wilson.

I knew Willie for only 20 years, so many others have an
advantage over me. I didn't know Willie when he was a cub
reporter in his native Dingwall. I didn't know him when he was a
danceband musician. I didn't know him when he was club
secretary to Ross County.

I knew him as a dedicated community fund-raiser, a most
considerate and thoughtful colleague and, above all, as the best
story-teller and natural comedian I have had the privilege to meet.

I have seen an entire function suite of grown men and women
crying with laughter and thumping tables, gasping for breath, on
hearing Willie tell the story about the chimpanzee who supported
Rangers.

And always Willie would stand there, deadpan, yet working the audience with a professional's expertise.

I was once in his company when someone foolishly suggested a joke-telling marathon. The rules were simple: round the table, one by one, 20 dinner guests had to tell a joke and draw genuine laughter. Then we would go round again. And again. Those who failed to get a laugh, or who could not think of a fresh joke, had to retire defeated. Ultimately, only one joker would be left.

You don't need me to tell you who won more than two hours later, and still he looked as if he was barely out of first gear.

Most remarkably of all, Willie would receive joke requests. He could, and did, tell the same story several times to the same people at many different functions and still wow the crowds into the same hysteria he had generated at first telling.

It really was the way he told them.

You heard Willie before you saw him. His trademark cackle carried far ahead of him. And always the reaction in the room was the same. People would look up, smiling, knowing who was coming. When he appeared in any room, he would clap backs, shake hands and peck the ladies on the cheek, adding in his Ross-shire accent: "Hello, darleen. It's yourself."

Everyone would be beaming. I remember wondering if I knew anyone else who was so well liked in so many places. I don't think I do.

When my first book was published, Willie was on the phone that night to offer congratulations and a gentle critique. He said he had heard that I would be doing a reading and a signing session in Inverness a couple of weeks later and hoped that he would find time to be there.

He finished by recommending a place for lunch (instructing me to mention his name), and observing that he had no doubt that very shortly I would have hordes at my heels wanting autographs.

Willie didn't make it to the reading and signing; the pull of his beloved Ross County was too strong. But I was sitting quietly in his recommended restaurant, gathering my thoughts for the reading and signing session, when three women, probably sisters in their 50s, approached tentatively.

One leaned over the table. "Are you the man who writes in The Press and Journal?"

I looked up. "Em, yes."

"The one who's written a book?"

"Yeeeeeeees."

She turned to the two others.

"I knew it. I just knew it." She turned back. "We're awful sorry to spoil your lunch but, I wonder, would you mind just signing your name on the tops of our Press and Journals?" I must have looked wary, for she added quickly: "You'll make our day."

I'll admit to the most fleeting and sneaking suspicion, never having been asked for an autograph before (or since), but I took out my pen and signed the mastheads. Off went the three ladies, quite contented.

It was weeks later that Willie confessed that he had set me up; that the three women hadn't known me from Jock the Coalman, and that they were neighbours of his who shared his keenness for a joke. "But I did warn you you'd have autograph hunters after you," he said.

Willie had a remarkable gift for getting on with everyone. I don't think I knew a more social or sociable man. I have attended functions in all sorts of company, from the humblest community events to the most imposing national conferences, and always someone would ask what Willie was up to.

He had an enviable knack of relating equally well to the wee pensioner widow and to the captains of British industry. Willie's contacts among the movers and shakers of the United Kingdom would astonish Dingwall, which knew him simply as the cheery man who penned a chatty column in the local weekly; who compered fund-raising events, and who had Ross County engraved on his heart.

Yet his close personal friends included a past chairman of Ford of Britain and two leading national politicians. When news of his illness broke, one senior British-industry executive jumped on a plane within an hour of hearing and flew from London to visit him.

That was the measure of the regard in which Willie was held.

His gregarious spirit led him into many embarrassing situations, he once told me. The only one he detailed concerned a Moray woman he had met briefly at a function in Inverness.

Months later, he was marching through Heathrow when he spied the same woman sitting alone on a seat. He sat down next to her and put a jokey arm round her. "Hullo darleen," he said. "Are you do-een anytheen tonight?"

He regretted his mateyness even before the words were out of his mouth, for the woman looked half-terrified. It was the first time that someone had met Willie Wilson and, within months, had forgotten who he was.

Willie died on Sunday after a year's battle against cancer. He was only 64.

As everyone expected, he bore the latter stages of his illness with great dignity and his customary good humour.

Two colleagues travelled from Glasgow to visit him in hospital. They arrived at his bedside to find him chatting up the nurses, as was his custom, and with none of the demeanour and gloom that the two had expected of a terminal patient.

"How's it gaun, Willie?" asked one.

"Well, put it this way," said Willie, beaming, "I'm not starting any long books."

Willie's funeral will be held tomorrow. Dingwall will not have seen a funeral quite like it.

I'm sure that his wife, Margaret, daughter Lorraine, son Willie and his grandchildren will be comforted, perhaps even astonished, by the evidence of the breadth and depth of respect and regard that Willie enjoyed; not just in Ross-shire, but throughout the country. Many faces in the assembly will be strangers in Easter Ross.

For myself, I am sorry that we have lost him, because he was far too good to lose, but I am pleased that he is not in pain any longer.

I have a tantalising mental image of him, holding court in a far better place, telling the joke about the chimpanzee who happened to be a Rangers devotee, and drawing howls of laughter.

And as long as we're still laughing, he's not so far away.

10. COPING WITH THE BRAT PACK

Or why indulging little monsters only produces big monsters

"If you don't sit down and behave, I'm going to kick your backside twice around the garden, tie you to a tree and let wild animals come and eat you in the night."

THE Audi was still only bowling up our drive when I had the first forebodings of doom. I could feel it in my bones. Something was rotten in Aberdeenshire. Then the car doors opened and out they tumbled. Mum, Dad and Three Demons from Hell, aged five, four and two. They scanned the grounds with malevolent eye for a few moments, then ran up and stared at me as I stood on the doorstep trying to look welcoming.

Mum and dad were friends of Mrs Harper, so she was pleased to see them. That was fine. But we hadn't been prepared for the band of diminutive hooligans they had brought in tow.

"This is Colin. This is Peter. And this is Michael." We eyed each other up and down and the dislike was instant and mutual. Then they pushed past me, uninvited, determined to explore the house.

The chill tightened even more when dad hauled a large portmanteau of toys from the boot and asked brightly: "Is there somewhere acceptable for them to play with their toys?"

"Out on the main road," I muttered, and got a short jab in the small of the back from my wife, who smiled broadly and trilled: "Come in, come in."

We went upstairs to the sitting-room and sat down. The bag of toys was dumped at the top of the stairs, while we adults sat down for a chat. When the three brutes disappeared for a few moments and it went too quiet, I'll admit to becoming worried, but then they reappeared, flushed, laughing — and soaking.

"Mummy! There's a founting in the bedroom."

"A founting?" I thought.

I got up and went to the far end of our house and our bedroom. They had broken in, made their way to the en-suite and had evidently had a high old time with the bidet. Everything was soaking — rugs, towels, walls, cosmetics, toiletries. The lot.

By the time I got back, the tea things were out. Colin had his ugly little face hard against an expensive Italian lamp, tiny fingers straining to reach it. I put it higher. Peter was trying to plunge the coffee filter and I wanted to let him, half-hoping it would blow back on him. Michael had found his way into my study; had spotted the word-processor, and was jumping up trying to batter the keys. I ushered him out and shut the door.

Colin was now propelling toys along the landing and clapping his hands with delight as they battered into the new skirting and unblemished doors. Peter was running along the lobby, dragging his grubby fingers along pristine walls. I tugged his arm away. He looked up at me, furious.

Our exchange of glances spoke volumes. His said: "Who do think you are, laying a finger on me?"

And mine said: "If you don't sit down and behave, I'm going to kick your backside twice around the garden, tie you to a tree and let wild animals come and eat you in the night."

I went back into the sitting-room, where the parents were chatting, quite unconcerned by their List D brood. As coffee was served, Michael appeared as if from nowhere and stretched a hand towards the plate of chocolate biscuits.

"Michael, you know you're not allowed to eat chocolate," said his mother. Michael withdrew strategically and played with his toys for a few moments, but the little eyes always drifted back to the plate of chocolate biscuits.

After a few minutes, he laid aside his toy quietly, then stood up and sauntered back on a wavy, idle sort of trajectory, as if merciful fate was leading him, quite by chance, towards the Kit-Kats.

Within striking distance, when he felt we were sufficiently engrossed in the conversation, the little hand slipped down towards the Kit-Kats, and then:

"Michael, I've said already. No chocolate."

And Michael grabbed a teaspoon instead, screamed and howled with the rage of a thousand demons and hurled the spoon at the centre of the tray of tea things. That teaspoon hit a crystal glass and smashed it into three dozen bits.

We all stared at the smashed glass. Michael, meanwhile, turned on his heels and stamped off in the huff. Slowly, I looked up at the parents and waited.

Now here's a test. What would you, as a parent, have done?

A: Leaped out of your seat, heated his backside and brought him back to apologise.

B: Leaped out of your seat, heated his backside and brought him back to apologise, and apologise yourself.

C: Leaped out of your seat, taken him across to a corner, heated his backside in privacy, apologise and offer to pay for the glass.

This is what actually happened: the parents looked at the glass. I looked at the parents. They looked back, mildly embarrassed. I carried on staring at them, waiting for an appropriate action.

Then, almost shamed into doing something, the mother turned and called after him: "Michael, that was naughty."

And that was it. I waited for more-tangible evidence of our displeasure and the gravity of his sin, but it didn't come. Instead, she picked up her coffee cup and the threads of the conversation and the incident was apparently closed.

What a naughty Michael.

I sat and fumed, debating inwardly whether or not to say something crisp or whether or not to write out a bill for damages.

And, if you'll excuse me, that was why I despaired on reading this week that Epoch, the children's rights group, are on their soapbox again wanting to ban physical punishment of children.

No one willingly raises a hand to children, but some brats are already so far out of line, even at pre-school age, that even the most right-on parents have to abandon higher principles, bite the bullet and do the unthinkable.

Start the upbringing determined to be violence-free, by all means. If it works, I'm delighted for you. If it doesn't — and the chances are it won't because a child's nature is to test you by pushing at the boundaries of behaviour and noting your reactions — don't be frightened of a swift stinging smack on the back of the legs or the behind, just as last-resort persuasion. Nothing more. Just make it quick and make sure the child knows why.

Your short-term guilt will be rewarded, long-term, by socially adjusted adults with respect for others, the rights of others and for others' property.

And no, it isn't enough to claim blithely that you can discipline children by reasoning with them. A six-year-old is incapable of reason. You cannot expect it of him.

In 10 years, the couple who visited us will be on the edges of nervous breakdowns as their hooligan sons run riot. In 15, they'll be sitting on their sofas providing character references to social workers.

But they'll have the satisfaction of knowing that professional namby-pambies will be able to smile indulgently, while thugs spit at our feet in the street and bricks whistle round our heads and coo: "Ooh, that was naughty."

Some colleagues couldn't believe that I would write so harshly about friends of Mrs Harper, knowing that they might read it and take offence.

But why not?

Everything in this column was exactly as it happened, apart from the fact that I fumed and stewed about such appalling parenting for days. They haven't been back.

11. CHILD ABUSE AND EATING OUT

Or why not to have an early meal in a family pub

▬ ▬ ▬ ▬

"She was a picture: white stilettos, caked in Max Factor,
gipsy-hoop earrings, raven-dyed hair, and a skirt so short
that she almost had two more cheeks to powder."

IT HAS been a delinquent week in the howe. Well, not strictly speaking in the howe, for we decided on Saturday afternoon to become part of the national revival in cinemagoing and spend a night at the pictures.

More than that, we decided to paint the town red and have a tuna softie and diet cola in advance at an eatery on the outskirts of Aberdeen.

Even better, we decided, if time permitted, to have a quick stroll round the shops of the top end of Union Street. Life is just a merry-go-round.

There was still heat in the afternoon by the time we reached Little Chelsea. We stopped at a few windows and wondered at people who pay silly money for desperately ordinary garments with a rather dowdy check when they could strap a neon sign above their heads flashing M-U-G.

And that was when we heard the sounds of a little person crying. We strolled tentatively round the corner trying to pretend we weren't really interested and there, cowering in a shop doorway, looking very small and vulnerable, was a beautiful little girl of about six, who might have stepped off a chocolate-box lid or out of an advertisement for Pears Soap.

She had long, shiny blonde hair done up in ribbons, and wore a floral-print dress and little white sandals.

And she was sobbing.

Over her stood a woman in her mid-twenties, whom we took to be her mother, wearing Doc Marten boots, a long print skirt and a black T-shirt. And she was shouting.

"No McDonalds, Kylie! Forget it! No McDonalds!" It was high-decibel, foghorn stuff.

So we smiled to ourselves as we sauntered on, for the lure of a cheeseburger in a brightly coloured restaurant is strong when you're only six. But then we heard: "No McDonalds! Pick somewye else or - - - - off!"

We looked at each other.

"Did I just hear . . . ?"

". . . I think you did."

As we walked on, aghast, to Holburn Junction and the car, I couldn't help recalling another incident, from 1986 or thereabouts, in much the same part of town at much the same time of day. I was alone and walking to the junction.

Towards me was striding a young man in his early twenties, half-shaven but sharp haircut, and dressed in denim. Four or five yards behind him waddled a wee lad with the tell-tale bulge of nappies under his dungarees; his tongue resolutely out at the side of his mouth and a determined stare on his face as he did his best to keep up.

Then the man turned. Sharply.

The wee lad tripped to a halt with the fright of it. The man grabbed the toddler by handfuls of jersey and dungaree straps and jerked him off the ground until their faces were level. The little lad's feet were dangling four feet off the ground.

The man said: "I've telt ye already! You - - - - - - - keep up or I'll rin awa and leave ye!"

You won't be surprised to know that the toddler was howling long before he was dropped to the pavement again.

There might be a common denominator here.

Either the top end of Union Street on a Saturday afternoon is to be avoided by all toddlers and little girls who know what is best for them, or the parenting skills of some young mums and dads are lacking.

We'll never know what stresses and strains the young woman and young man had weathered after a hot day's shopping with tired children, but there seems very little call to treat small people that way.

You'll excuse the armchair sociology, but if the fault lies in the parenting skills and not in Union Street, is it unfair to suppose that certain six-year-olds and 12-year-olds swear explosively and have no regards for the rights and morals of others because their own rights and morals have been violated from such a tender age?

The scene shifts now to our pre-cinema softie and cola in one of those family pub-restaurants which have sprung up on the outskirts of every British city in the last five years.

We had been dining peacefully in a little alcove next to an empty table, when suddenly, with great commotion, a small dynasty descended upon us: three women in their thirties, a tired-looking man in his early forties and enough children to keep a small rural school viable for a decade and a half.

The oldest woman was a picture. White stilettos. Caked in Max Factor. Gipsy-hoop earrings. Raven-dyed hair. A skirt so short that she almost had two more cheeks to powder. All she needed was a set of lights and she'd have been a Christmas tree.

And she was chewing gum. Worse, like many people, she was evidently unable to shut her mouth while doing so.

"Darren, fi' are yez wintin?" she shouted at one of the boys (chaw-chaw-chaw). Her two female companions, equally bedecked, took out their fags and lit up.

Darren, meanwhile, was studying our softies disdainfully. "Nae sangwidges, onywye," said Darren, his face all sotters and dried tomato ketchup.

"Well, fi' yez wintin? (chaw-chaw-chaw) D'yez wint a curry? D'yez wint a baked ta''ie? Praan salad? Fi' yez wintin?"

Darren, meanwhile, jumped on to one of the seats with his filthy feet and began peering round the room.

An older girl, her index finger rammed up her nose to the third knuckle, let it be known that she would like "a burger and chups"

Then the cry from all eight juveniles went up: "Bur-gers! Bur-gers! Bur-gers!"

We sat, sipping our diet colas delicately, mesmerised at the performance which goes into getting a squad of offspring settled. It took fully 10 minutes. Half of them went out on to the terrace to shout and chase the swans, while four others stayed in to whine about being hot and bored.

The adults settled themselves with their drinks and fags and began a conversation about their night out, the new car one of their friends had bought and how Christmas was getting closer.

Then the earrings woman said: "Darren's go' a le"er hame fae his school (chaw-chaw-chaw). The heidie says there's folk sellin drugs at the school gates. He's says the kids is in danger. At a primary school! Drugs! Zatny affa?

"Saffa that," said the three other adults.

"It amazes ye, dis it?" said Earrings, now in full oratorical flow. "How could folk dee that tae little kids? They're sick. They need lockin up. (chaw-chaw-chaw) 'At's abuse, 'at. Nae much wonder there's crime. Child abuse is fit that is."

And then a very bored Darren pushed her petulantly in the small of her back.

She spun round.

"Darren! For - - - -'s sake behave yersel or I'll ba"er ye!"

━━ ━━ ━━ ━━

Several people wondered if the punchline to this column was true or if I had embellished it.

As Mrs Harper will attest, it was 100% accurate, and we had a hard time not laughing.

The other question was: "Where was this restaurant?" Let's just say it's on a major junction south out of Aberdeen. We haven't been back.

12. AN EDINBURGH FAUX-PAS

Or why it's a good idea to watch your step in a department store

——— ——— ——— ———

*"Never tell me that age brings calm, contentment and
sweetness of temper. These were beings possessed, with
only one thing on their minds: the Early Bird Breakfast."*

IT HAS been a capitulationary week in the howe. That was
why we came to be tramping along Princes Street, Edinburgh,
on Saturday morning at 9am, bearing with great fortitude the
entire meteorological gamut of blizzards, howling gales, driving
rain and unseasonal sunshine in just the 25 minutes it took to
saunter from the GPO to the Caledonian Hotel.

It was for temporary respite from the elements that we took
shelter in the hallowed halls of Jenners, the grand department
store which basks in its status as the best-known name on
Scotland's best-known street.

Jenners is a strange mix of the traditional and the contemporary.
It employs up-to-date marketing and display techniques, yet it
does it in a wood-panelled and alabaster atmosphere which
breathes softly of affluence and heritage and blue-rinsed matrons
of Newington and Morningside.

It is stores such as Jenners that tax the vigilance of all men. You
cannot afford to let your concentration slip for an instant. On
Saturday, for instance, I might easily have been duped into a
department called Summer Separates, from which escape would
have been impossible, except through Co-ordinates or past New
for Spring, which would have been just as bad.

The spousely psychology employed on these occasions is instructive. Norman Schwarzkopf could take lessons in military strategy from any shopping Scotswoman.

My wife, for example, has long given up on the direct approach, because she knows that gets her nowhere. Instead, when we enter a store, she stalks purposefully towards the back, where we wander deliberately past books and magazines, dallying just long enough to demonstrate that she is sharing my interest.

Then, I might find myself being sauntered past computers and photographic, where I am permitted another five minutes. Thence to music, or the patisserie or, even better, the toys.

Only then do surroundings become progressively unfamiliar. It begins innocuously enough. In your reverie, you half-notice that you are ambling past towels, tablecloths and duvets.

Gradually the towels and duvets become carpets and curtains. You look round for a point of reference, but there is none.

Then it's bathroom fitments followed by the sickly sweetness of pot-pourri. Increasingly bewildered and disorientated, the unwary male is accelerated into the perfumery, which rapidly becomes luggage and leather. Then Easter gifts. Haberdashery. Glassware. Scarves. Shoes.

And then . . .

BANG!

. . . the steel teeth of the trap are sprung and there you are:

Women's Clothes

Two hours of Aquascutum, Jaeger, Janet Reger, Viyella, Jacques Vert and Liz Claiborne. Sitting outside changing rooms. Trying not to look suicidal. And you have none but yourself to blame.

The seasoned male, on the other hand, is alert to these tawdry ploys. On Saturday, as soon as the towels and duvets began to appear, I formulated a plan.

By the time we got to carpets and curtains, I knew the set of her mind so, at Bathroom Fitments, I took evasive action and vectored off to Fine Porcelain, tacked through Beds and Beddings, doubled back at the Delicatessen from whence the trajectory termination was the fourth-floor restaurant, and breakfast.

She caught up with me a couple of minutes later looking slightly nonplussed and weary.

"I felt hungry," I explained. "I could do with coffee and toast."

"You'd better join the queue, then," she said. And I turned round to see a long line of Edinburgh's most affluent senior citizenry, waiting beside firmly closed restaurant doors. From the line drifted snatches of Morningside conversational trivia.

"Lovely morning, Mrs Gilfillan."

"Lovely, lovely morning, Miss Cruickshank. How have your pipes been after all that frost?"

"Never been better. Never been better. Had them checked over by a man my nephew knows. What he doesn't know about pipes is not worth knowing, let me tell you."

And on and on and on.

Clearly Jenners' Saturday-morning breakfast is part of the geriatric club ritual in Edinburgh, so we joined the queue. At once, we were surveyed by the gimlet eyes of two dozen pensioners. Their conversation quietened while they drank in us interlopers.

Then the doors opened. The melee caught us by surprise; the most spectacular thing outside a Murrayfield scrum. Scrawny necks, elbows and ankles disappeared in a blur as they hared towards the grub. Never tell me that age brings calm, contentment and sweetness of temper. These were beings possessed, with only one thing on their minds: the Early Bird Breakfast.

Like an RAF formation, half of them broke off to starboard to bag their usual tables, while their breakfast companions scuttled towards the servery and the aroma of gently sizzling bacon, sausage and tomato.

"I'll get us a table," said my wife and, in a smart manoeuvre, picked a plum location beside a picture window, with a view of Princes Street and the castle.

Bad move.

By the time I joined her with our two coffees, rack of toast and pastries, I could sense that something was wrong. We were being surveyed intently by the occupants of at least half a dozen tables.

I looked back and their stares snapped away instantly to their condiments, their laps — anything , in fact, except me.

Unexpected attention: check flies.

Secure on the spaver front. No parsley on my teeth. Shoes clean. Trouser seams still intact.

"I think," whispered my wife, "that we have taken someone's table."

And that, of course, was the answer. We'd had the effrontery to take a table customarily occupied first thing on a Saturday morning by Miss McTavish and Miss Morrison, or whatever their names were, presumably the two matrons all tweeds, brogues and hatpins, glowering from the queue at the till, fit to set us afire.

We ate our breakfast in defiance of custom and practice, but I can't pretend it was the most relaxing snack I have eaten. The whispers of outrage and hot glares from the regulars made it notably uncomfortable.

We left to intense inspection, pulling on our coats. As we departed, I looked back to see Miss McTavish and Miss Morrison reoccupying the high ground, acknowledging the admiring gazes of congratulation from their fellows.

And I, disorientated, bewildered, preoccupied and quite unsuspecting, was led away, by a mind far more cunning than mine, on the long and circuitous route to Women's Clothes.

I was contacted shortly after this column appeared in March, 1994, by the catering manager at Jenners who had enough of a sense of humour to invite us back to try an Early Bird breakfast in less intimidating surroundings.

I couldn't accept, of course, but we have returned to the store several times; just a little more careful to observe the finer points of restaurant etiquette.

13. IT WAS A DARK NIGHT AT THE HOTEL

Or why to keep clear of potato croquettes

___ ___ ___ ___

"With fork and spoon at a jaunty angle, I chased every
one of those croquettes round and round the platter until
two spun off and landed in the man's lap."

IT HAS been a tiffinesque week in the howe. The diets begun so nobly after New Year were shoogled just a little by a Saturday gastronomic tour of Badenoch and Strathspey.

Badenoch and Strathspey?

Yes, Badenoch and Strathspey

The jewel of the Central Highlands might not be writ in flame on Egon Ronay's heart, but he hasn't had banoffi pie at the Ecclefechan Bistro, Carrbridge.

Gastronomy at that stretch of the River Dulnain has come a long way in the 20 years since I had a post-school summer job at one of the area's largest hotels.

While Chef fought to turn out meals which reflected credit on his profession, and which he hoped would light up the fading eyes of coachloads of octogenarians ferried from the North of England courtesy of Wallace Arnold, he was sadly let down by elements on his staff.

The rogue elements were such as the commis chef who was a little more avant garde than even Egon Ronay would have liked. When one evening the larder ran out of mint sprigs for the boiled potatoes, he had a brainwave and tipped half a jar of mint sauce into the gently hottering water.

For the rest of the evening, waiters and waitresses had to explain why the potatoes were a fetching shade of Irish Green. They spun some lame story about it being a new strain of Gaelic spud, bred for a taste of the Highlands, an interesting appearance and its conversation-stopping potential when presented in a vegetable medley with Kerr's Pinks.

It was the same commis chef who, challenged by a harassed hotel porter to produce bacon sandwiches for two hungry businessmen in a tremendous hurry, rose to the occasion with a style not seen since the days of Escoffier.

Howls of anguish from the front lounge five minutes later sent the porter back, in the interests of customer care, to find out what might be the problem.

"The problem, laddie," said one businessman, "is that we prefer the bacon cooked."

Even I was guilty one evening. A commercial traveller had phoned ahead to say that he would be arriving late, possibly around midnight, but would it be possible for him to have a hot meal?

Chef and the kitchen staff were alerted, but pointed out that they would be long gone by midnight, nursing a well-earned dram in their bosies and their feet up in front of the TV.

However, Chef took sufficient pity on me to set up everything so that I could do duty as chef, waiter and sommelier, all in one.

"It's idiot-proof," he said. "I've assembled a paté starter, a ham salad for main course and you can get some ice-cream in the freezer."

"But he wants a hot meal."

Chef rolled his eyes. "So you make him toast for the paté, and you give him hot potato croquettes with the salad. Are you up to that?"

"Maybe," I said, knowing I was lying.

"It's easy," he said. "The toast for the paté's a doddle and we'll leave the deep-fat frier on, with three croquettes in the basket. As soon as you've served the paté, come back and lower the basket into the fat for precisely three minutes.

"And then put them on the plate?"

"Certainly not. This is a good client. He'll expect silver service."

"What? All that business with a fork and spoon in one hand?"

"Absolutely."

And off they went.

If ever you have sat in a deserted hotel kitchen at night, you'll know that few eerier places exist. Every noise from every end of every room and corridor bangs, rumbles and echoes as equipment cools down and thermostats switch on and off. It is not a place for those of a profoundly feart disposition.

I whiled away the time whistling to keep up my spirits and counting the potato croquettes every so often. I'm not sure where I expected them to go but, comfortingly, they stayed exactly where they were.

I spent a few minutes picking what I imagined were sufficiently aesthetic slices of Co-opie loaf for the toast. Then I waited.

It was on the dot of midnight that the man arrived, tired, bedraggled and drawn. I showed him to his room; asked when he would like his meal, and he said he'd be down in five minutes.

"No problem," I said, and I bounded back downstairs to shove the bread under the gas grill. I removed the protective plate from the paté and took the concoction to the dining-room to await our late diner.

I ran back to the kitchen, praying that the toast hadn't burned. It hadn't. Though I say it myself, those were probably the finest slices of toast in the annals of the western hemisphere. I cut the crusts, sliced the toast into triangles, arranged them daintily and took them through in time to meet the diner fluffing out his napkin.

"I'd hoped for a hot meal," he said, eyeing the paté sadly.

"And here's your toast," I said with a flourish. He couldn't have had the heart to object.

I raced back to the kitchen and dipped the croquette basket into the frier.

That was when my luck started to unravel. I still don't know what went wrong, or if Chef had played a joke on me, but there was a sudden thrashing and boiling of the fat. It foamed brilliant white; cracked, banged and spat at me, and then, when this adipose maelstrom subsided 30 seconds later, I was the proud beholder of three cylinders of crisp Ruskoline completely devoid of content.

Empty.

No potato; just croquette.

This was a major predicament. The man wanted a hot meal and the only hot things I had now were empty croquette shells. Beautifully golden, mark you, but with no potato inside.

What to do? I brazened it out. I tipped the three shells on to a silver platter, arranged a slice of lettuce and two quarter-tomatoes as best I could, and proudly bore my creation to the dining-room.

I might have got away with it but for my lack of dexterity at silver service. With fork and spoon at a jaunty angle between fingers quivering with tension, I chased every one of those croquettes round and round the platter until two spun off and landed in the man's lap.

He looked at me. I looked at him. He looked at the croquettes. And then, gingerly, I tried to pick them up — silver service.

I still don't know what I captured between that fork and spoon, but it didn't sound like croquettes.

I don't think we ever saw him again.

Whenever I have been stuck for inspiration for a column, casting my mind back to the summer of 1975 and my summer job at that hotel has rescued me.

I have said before that it was like living 24 hours a day in a sitcom. Such bizarre things happened that, even now, I find it hard to believe that the place made any money at all.

14. LAND OF THE FOUNTAIN AND THE FLOOD

Or why it's a good idea to keep your temper over simple mistakes

"Here was a woman used to being assertive and obeyed.
Here was a woman used to getting her own way.
She had to be a teacher."

IT HAS been a penitent week in the howe. Some people manage to hold on to holiday friendships for years; decades even. We have been unable to maintain one beyond a handful of days, mainly because we don't know her name.

Our accommodation in the Algarve earlier this month had all the charm of the St Fergus gas terminal; a bleak spread of concrete, steel and whistling gales. Apart from hiring a car and travelling as far from the place as frequently as possible, the only respite was our neighbour across the landing.

On the afternoon of our arrival, still in shock after seeing our billet for the first time, we had heard raised voices across the hall. From the volume, the occupant of the apartment opposite was standing in the corridor and conducting an efficient verbal assault on a member of staff. The complaints were legion and detailed, ranging from the state of the towels to the lack of power sockets to the distance from the lift. From the timbre of the voice, she was an elderly lady and very, very English.

Since I'm not so nosy as to fling open the door and savour other people's disagreements, I peeped through our keyhole. The line of vision was wrong, so all that I saw was a bulging midriff, tweedy skirt and cosy stockings leading to sensible shoes. "We're living opposite Margaret Rutherford," I advised the CO, who advised in turn that I leave the door and mind my own business.

Then, with a sharp: "I shall expect matters put right by this evening," Miss Rutherford shochled round and closed her door not with a slam but with surprising grace. There had been no need for an "or else"; the tone of voice had been sufficient. Here was a woman used to being assertive and obeyed. Here was a woman used to getting her own way.

She had to be a teacher.

The first time I met "Miss Rutherford" was the day Cell Block H's water supply had failed at dawn and we had been advised that repair would take some time. After a morning on the beach and a post-lunch flopdown on the bed, I awoke in late afternoon, swung my legs out and, splash, found myself ankle-deep in water.

The landing was awash and the source was Miss Rutherford's apartment. I knocked sharply at her door once or twice to little effect and then hared down to Reception and suggested that they send up some staff. On the way back, shochling along the corridor, and leaning heavily on a walking-stick, was a figure clothed in tweed skirt and sensible shoes.

"Excuse me," I said, talking from a distance so as not to frighten her, "are you in room three-two-six?"

"Yes, I am. I've been downstairs for tea. It was disgraceful."

"I'm sorry to say your apartment appears to be flooding. I think you might have left the taps open this morning when the water was off. The supply has been connected again, so the water has been gushing everywhere. My wife and I are two inches deep, our luggage is soaking and the water is half-way along the landing."

She seemed to swoon for a moment, then we turned the corner and she stopped to behold Lake Tanganyika, spreading steadily towards us along the lobby tiles.

"Oh, my," she said. "I've never done anything like this before. What on earth was I thinking of?"

It is very difficult to be patient, even with an elderly person, when water is rising towards power sockets and your feet are soaking. "Do you think you could go into your room and turn off the taps?" I said.

"How on earth could that have happened?"

"It might be an idea to switch off the water."

"Such a dreadful mess. Are your things badly damaged?"

"Not so far. Could you go in and switch off the water, please?"

"We should get a man up."

"He's coming."

So she gave me her key and I switched off both bath taps, a sink tap and a kitchen tap and returned to escort her through to her sofa. At that, we were joined by the CO.

"I am most dreadfully sorry," said Miss Rutherford. "Never have I done such a thing in all my years of travelling."

And, very softly, she began to cry.

"Now, now, now," said the CO, sitting down beside her and offering a hankie. "No damage has been done. It's a tile floor and it's only water. Anyone could have made the same mistake.

"Please let me compensate you," she sobbed. "How much damage do you think I have done?"

"No compensation needed," I said. "Everything will dry out."

"My daughter will be so angry."

"When is she due back?"

"She's not in Portugal yet. I'm on my own, you see." She began sobbing again, and the CO suggested with a glance and a gesture that I make them a cup of tea. Sobbing women are not my forte.

While an odd-job boy and I mopped up the flood, the CO sat with Miss Rutherford and heard a life story of incredible sadness. She had been a primary headmistress in Essex. It was a small school, but a good one, until councillors had decided to rationalise and had closed it down with a month's notice.

She had been given a learning-support post in a nearby secondary school, but professional satisfaction and pride had been extinguished and she had retired at 55 on a small pension.

Her husband had left her after 15 years of marriage, and she had brought up a son and a daughter. The daughter was good to her and kept in touch, but she had not seen her son in more than 35 years; a sorrow she bore privately.

Now, she scrimped and saved a few pounds from her pension while she stayed in Britain in the summers so that she could afford long-term holidays round the Mediterranean in winter. Sometimes, her daughter joined her, but mostly she was on her own.

The CO thought that Miss Rutherford was not visibly enjoying her holiday. She was out of breath, walking painfully and deeply tired. Solitude hung heavily about her. She was 85.

We saw Miss Rutherford only once more in our week. We met one morning as we headed out for a walk and she was returning from breakfast. She took a few moments to recognise us, then began apologising again for the flood. We changed the subject and spoke of the weather and the markets, and she spoke of feeling a little unwell, although she insisted it was nothing to worry about.

After five minutes, as we turned to go, she stopped us and said something that seared through me as I began walking away.

She said: "Thank you for speaking to me."

That night, as we returned to the hotel, we saw an ambulance leaving. Reception could not say who had been in the ambulance. None of the tour reps was responsible for the occupant of Room 326, and there was no reply at the door for the remaining two days of her holiday.

We hope she is well.

We never did establish if "Miss Rutherford" survived her holiday or if her daughter treated her kindly.

I can say honestly that I have rarely felt sorrier for someone who had made a simple mistake and who was needlessly contrite, nor felt more of a flash of heat go through me at the poignancy of her Parthian shot.

15. EVERY PENNY A PRISONER

Or a dozen ways to save yourself half-a-croon

━━ ━━ ━━ ━━

A Huntly man sat each evening carefully splitting every
match from a box of Swan Vestas. Once each had been
split lengthways, he had twice the number of matches.

IT HAS been a parsimonious week in the howe. I have been
leafing through all your tales of thrift and frugality, and pretty
sobering reading it made. You might remember that a few
weeks ago I recounted stories of a man who went to the trouble
of calculating that it was cheaper to light a fire with a lighter than
with matches.

I went on to mention the worker who gave his colleagues a lift
home every evening, but stopped a couple of hundred yards short
of their homes one night. When his passengers asked why, he
reminded them that the Chancellor of the Exchequer had put up
the price of petrol that day. Consequently, that was as far as they
were going on what they had chipped in to the petrol kitty.

And we finished with the man who, allegedly, switched off the
gas every time he turned a rasher of bacon in the pan.

"Top that," we said. You took up the challenge beautifully, and
the fax machines duly started before 9am on the day of
publication as dozens of you strove to better our examples.

Whether or not all the following tales are genuine is up to you.
Since we are dealing with Press and Journal readers here, I
suspect a heavy measure of tongue in cheek in some of them.
Others have a horrible ring of truth.

I liked the faxed (anonymous) message from an oil company in Peterhead in which they told me that one of the senior managers had made a habit of going into the canteen and asking: "How much for a couple of butteries?"

"40p."

"And how much for one?"

"25p."

"I'll tak the ither een."

John Smith (not his real name), of Culter (not his real location), was extremely concerned that his identity did not leak, for the subject of his letter was still alive, he said, and he didn't want to risk the friendship.

The man, apparently, was seen walking downstairs with his legs wide apart. After two or three such circuits, John asked him why he was walking downstairs in such an odd manner.

"Ye dinna weer oot the carpet in the same place," said the man. And that was in somebody else's house.

Someone from the Banffshire coast, who also asked not to be named, reminded me of the extra gear on cars sold in Scotland. There's first, second, third, fourth, fifth, reverse — and Aberdeen Overdrive.

Aberdeen Overdrive is freewheeling downhill.

The same correspondent told a tale of a Huntly man who sat by the light of the fire each evening carefully splitting each match from a box of Swan Vestas. Once every match had been split lengthways, he had twice the number of matches.

We had two tales from separate parts of Caithness, and one from Banffshire, of husbands who switch off the car's wipers when they pass under a bridge.

I liked the story from Stuart Watson, of Inverurie, who reported (with a straight face, I presume, Stuart) that when he got his first pair of spectacles his father made him take them off when he wasn't looking at anything in particular.

David Smith, of Anstruther, cast his mind back to 1946, when he started as a boy cook on a St Monans herring drifter, sailing out of the Broch.

One of the crew had a weekly shave with an open razor, which he sharpened on a leather strap. After each shave, he wrapped up his soap brush unrinsed so that it would do the following week.

Willie Smith, of Foggieloan, claimed to have spotted a friend of his filling up with petrol, taking a paper hankie to soak up the drops from the rubber overspill well, then squeezing the drops back into the tank.

Bill Taylor, of Alness, wrote on the back of an old gas-supply application form (there's thrift for you) about the farmer who never used the farmhouse toilet but preferred to visit the midden. When challenged, he would always reply:

"Every little helps."

We had more than a dozen stories of husbands and fathers who drove on sidelights even in the darkest or foggiest conditions "because it saves the battery".

Two wives wrote plaintively about their garden sheds being temples to parsimony, packed with decades of rusting saw blades, oily ropes, perished rubber bath plugs, snapped spades, burst bicycle tyres, broken food-mixers, wizened wellies, boxes of assorted round-pin plugs, 1960s lampshades, wicker shopping baskets with more hole than wicker, long-dead car batteries and dozens of other defunct items, all stored by husbands who live by the maxim: "But you never know when these things will come in handy."

I admired the ingenuity of the correspondent who didn't finish his story. It ran out before the punchline with a wee note: "This is all the paper I could scrounge and now they want the pen back."

There were also a couple of stories which had the faint whiff of music-hall jokery, as in: The stage manager at the Tivoli in Aberdeen went on-stage at the end of the first half of the show. "Ladies and gentlemen, a sixpence has been found in one of the toilets. Would whoever lost it please form a queue at the ticket office?"

Or: "What's the definition of an Aberdonian visitor?"

"Someone with racing colours on his knife and fork."

Or the secretary to an Aberdeen joiner who disturbs him in his office. "Excuse me, there's a mannie at the door needin tae see ye."

"Nae wi a bill, I hope."

"No, a nose like aabody else."

But my favourite — and the one which wins a bottle of something tasty — was from an anonymous shopkeeper, I think, from the clues in his covering letter. If he cares to write again with his full name and address (and I promise to keep it secret) we'll send on the bottle.

He told of a young man who lived with his mother and father in a Banffshire town who had a substantial pools win. The young chap received his six-figure cheque and duly cashed it at the bank.

Once back home, he counted the money twice to make sure it was all there and, having satisfied himself, turned to his mother and father who were sitting on the settee watching him and threw them a fiver each.

His father studied the £5 note and asked what the son was thinking of doing with the rest of the money. His son replied that he thought he would find himself a girl and get married.

His father wasn't sure that that was at all necessary, because, after all: "I nivver mairriet yer mither."

The son was shocked and became agitated by this revelation. "But that maks me a b*******!"

"Aye," said the father, "and ye're a greedy b********, as weel."

The twist to this column was that, after dealing at length with parsimony and the delights of getting something for nothing, the winner of the bottle of whisky never did claim his prize. It's still sitting in the back of a cupboard behind my desk at the Lang Stracht.

And, no, it's not up for claiming any more.

16. BIRTHDAY GIRL

Or why it's important to spread a little sunshine at the superstore

---

"We trundled towards the revolving doors; she sitting in
the wheelchair determined to go left, and I pushing the
wheelchair pushing the trolley, insisting that we go right."

IT HAS been a complaisant week in the howe. For anyone who has endured surly service, or who has left a store or a confrontation with a public servant feeling betrachled, bothered and bewildered, exploited and demeaned, incandescent with fury, read on. This will cheer you up.

We spent Saturday celebrating, albeit a little belatedly, my mother-in-law's birthday. I am instructed not to reveal which birthday, but if you multiply 71 by 6 and divide the result by 2x3, you're not far off.

Since she is disabled and housebound — apart from trips to hospital in the back of an ambulance — we like to take her for a wee traivel on a summer Saturday just to blow the cobwebs off her.

These have not always met with clarion success. The big outing last year was marred by the birthday girl announcing — after we had spent a day driving up Deeside's most majestic scenery, across the stark moors of Glen Gairn and down the rolling hills of Donside, stopping to watch gliders taking off and landing, pausing to savour the majesty of a marchpast by a pipe band, finishing with a tour of the Aberdeen seaboard, the shipping in the Harbour and out to Girdleness and the vista of the North Sea — that she had left her glasses at home but she was sure that it had all looked really lovely.

This year, glasses rammed firmly on lugs, we opted for Deeside as far as Banchory, then up Feughside, over the Cairn o' Mount, pausing to view the spread of the Howe o' the Mearns, thence to Fettercairn for a snack and home by way of Stonehaven.

The coup de theatre, however, was to be a visit to a superstore; not whoop-de-do material to you and me, perhaps, but for someone who has been housebound for so many years, and has had to rely on others to do her messages, it was shaping up days in advance as the crown jewel.

We had phoned round in advance to find a store which provides wheelchairs for disabled customers and discovered, once we arrived, that not only did it offer wheelchairs free of charge, it had high-platform trolleys deigned specially to be held, manoeuvred and loaded by wheelchair customers.

If ever you have plonked someone in a wheelchair, and hooked up a full-size shopping trolley to the front of it before pushing into the Tower of Babel that is the modern, thronging superstore, you will understand the apprehension which stole over us. Like a small articulated vehicle, we trundled gingerly towards the revolving doors; she sitting in the wheelchair determined to go left, and I pushing the wheelchair pushing the trolley, insisting that we go right. Anyone who has reversed a caravan can see the flaw in this arrangement.

Superstore crowds are not of the sunniest of temperament at the best of times, but they seem particularly growly on a Saturday at teatime, when most customers want to be home cooking the chips, preparing for a night in front of the TV, or out on the tiles — anywhere except queueing with fractious children and harassed women and disgruntled husbands.

It did not bode well. As we broached the portals, the sea of scowls and girns, and howling bairns wanting sweeties, and barking mums threatening skelps and worse almost sent us back to the car.

But here's the surprise.

Pushing my mother-in-law was like pushing a time capsule of

courtesy. As someone who hasn't been out doing her own messages for nigh on 30 years, she is still a shopper of the past, untainted by the push-shove, get-oota-my-face, fa-are-you-lookin-at, I wis-here-first breed of modern city shopper.

She comes from an era when you smiled and passed the time of day and offered to let others with just short shopping lists go ahead of you.

"Lovely day," she beamed at the couple studying toothpaste as we bowled past the start of the first aisle. You'd have thought someone had passed a high-voltage current through their smalls.

We reached the fresh fruit and veg where a woman studying the melons was evidently unsure of their ripeness.

"Bananas look good the day," said my mother-in-law as I wheeled her past. The melon woman looked up, utterly mystified. You just don't talk to strangers in a superstore, but try telling that to a novice.

We reached Home Baking Requisites, where she began pulling out enough bags of currants, sultanas and raisins to halve the foreign debt of Greece. A young man, presumably waiting for his wife, was studying this trawling of soft fruit when my mother-in-law caught his gaze. "Ye canna be ower early wi yer Christmas puddings," she remonstrated.

As we were passing Spreads and Pastes, she noticed a woman poring over jars of beef paste, evidently labouring over a decision. Who better to help in such a quandary than Aberdeen's newest shopping consultant? "Three for the price of two on the salmon spread back there," she advised as she breezed past.

That was when we got the first thank-you and a smile. "Not at all," my mother-in-law called back, already rolling half-way to Jams and Jellies.

By the time we reached Household Cleaning, I was in half a mind to say something, but she was getting such favourable reaction wherever we went that I didn't like to. Up every aisle, down every aisle, she surprised customers with her cheery smile and comment mainly because she didn't know any differently.

And they returned it in kind. Far from grumbling at the slow-moving, trundling convoy of wheelchair-pusher, wheelchair,

wheelchair-occupant, trolley and enough groceries to keep a small town going for a wee nuclear holocaust, we were met with nothing but kindness, courtesy, assistance, smiles and cheery conversation from harassed fellow-customers and harried staff. There is a moral here for the rest of us.

The Does He Take Sugar? syndrome, in which well-meaning but unthinking people address questions meant for a disabled person to an able-bodied companion, as if physical disability addles the brain as well as the legs, was nowhere in evidence.

The woman at the delicatessen counter made a point of conversing directly with my mother-in-law, not with me, even although she could barely see her at the other side of the counter.

And as the last of the goods rang through the checkout, and she fumbled in her purse for her dues, she beamed up at the checkout operator.

"You know," she said, "that's the first time I've done my own shopping in 30 years."

"Well, I hope you enjoyed it," said the checkout lady.

The big beam on her face gave us the answer to that.

Well done, Tesco, Bridge of Don.

You couldn't have done better if you'd rolled out the red carpet.

The birthday girl is five years older now, but we have not been able to persuade her to return to a superstore.

By the time she got back home that day, she confessed that the last 90 minutes of her outing had been among the most exhausting of her whole life, which pretty much sums up my own attitude to superstore shopping, too.

17. LESSONS AT BREAKFAST

Or how to learn from puff-pastry politics

━━ ━━ ━━ ━━

"As I sat at breakfast each morning and watched the 20
delegates arrive, I witnessed all the interpersonal skills and
office politicking of British business in microcosm."

IT HAS been a recuperative week in the howe. Three weeks'
holiday pottering about at home can be just as draining as a
yomp around the Himalaya. Being Scandophiles, we had
intended to go to Denmark, but various appointments mitigated
against that, so we forsook Tivoli, Georg Jensen, Illums and the
Stroget and snatched a quick tour of the motor museums of
England.

If you don't like cars, you'll wonder at someone swapping
Wonderful Copenhagen, lutefisk and kjottboller for staring at
valves and pistons, but you won't understand until you've gazed
moistly at a Rover P4 in pristine condition, loved and tended since
birth with the respect she deserves.

We stayed at a country club and sports centre in the Midlands.
It had two golf courses, six tennis courts, a leisure pool, a
swimming pool, two restaurants, a health club, a sauna, a massage
parlour and various other places that involved being thumped,
bumped, rubbed, dubbed, creamed, steamed, slapped, clapped,
pummelled and walloped.

I avoided them all, for I can be thumped, pummelled and
walloped free of charge much nearer home. But the country club
mesmerised me almost as much as the motor museums. Nowhere

else had I seen such a proliferation of pot bellies and cellulite thighs all in the one place. The last time I came across that much orange peel was a hillside in Cyprus in 1984.

As an advert for a health club, it wasn't much of an advert. They shambled from the changing-rooms and slapped into the pool creating bow waves not seen since they sank the Bismarck. Business lunches have much to answer for.

Here and there, draped at strategic points around the poolside, were svelte, pouting young things in frosted lipstick and sporting low-cut, high-thighed, one-piece swimsuits which looked pretty much like two tangled ribbons.

But the intriguing part of the stay was the puff-pastry convention. Honestly. A convention for puff-pastry. A major manufacturer of puff-pastry was holding its 1993 sales convention at the health club. Puff-pushers from throughout Britain had converged on the health club to talk puff by day and huff and puff by night.

You might wonder about the choice of venue. Puff-pastryists at a health club is a bit like Pavarotti at a carrot-juice bar, or Hitler shopping at Mothercare. But there they were, more than 20 salespeople and marketeers, the nation's experts on rolling, shaping and fluting.

Had the chef hit an emergency with his steak-and-kidney, help was definitely at hand.

The really fascinating part was what sociologists would call Group Dynamics. As I sat at breakfast each morning and watched the 20 puff delegates arrive, I witnessed all the interpersonal skills and office politicking of British business in microcosm.

It went something like this:

Long before the main force came the vanguard of three or four tired old soldiers. Men in their 40s and 50s, they were still in the frontline after a lifetime on the road flogging shortcrust, choux and filo. No key to the executive toilet here. No advancement for years of loyalty, hard work and dedication.

They were what Americans would call PoPos (Pissed On and Pissed Off). They sat, tidy but rebelliously tieless, in a determined group at the far end of the long table; indifference and cynicism hanging heavily about them, unmoved by anything except the prospect of a good fry-up.

Next came the new recruits and the wimps. They arrived individually, not yet sufficiently convivial or co-ordinated to arrive in social groups.

They sat at the opposite end of the table from the PoPos, always with at least one space between them for privacy. They were dressed in new suits, one size too big, and shirts still with the tramlines and pinholes from the packet freshly opened only 20 minutes before. Most of them had wispy moustaches in an attempt to look older. It was a questionable policy, for it made most of them look like pre-school Zapatas.

They glanced around them nervously, smiling hopeful, empty smiles to people they didn't really know and who didn't care to know them. Between bites, they adjusted new ties, unable to eat much more than a chipolata and dry toast, thinking of their presentations later that morning and wondering if they had their slides in the right order.

Then there was a 20-minute lull, followed by a sudden rush of sharp suits. These were the Armani, Ralph Lauren, Boss brigade. Slickly coiffed and smoothly shod, they cruised in, impeccably fit and flash, laughing manufactured laughs through even teeth and all the while calculating whose back to stab next on their way to the top.

The PoPos looked up, sneered privately and went back to their bangers. The Wimps wondered if they should shift seats. The Armanis swept all before them, sitting where they chose, louder than anyone else with the brashness and arrogance of people still on the rise.

Next came the boss.

The chief executive ambled in, smiling avuncular smiles to all. The PoPos ignored it; the Wimps almost fainted at it, and the Armanis joked safe jokes with it.

Boss was trailed in close formation by the Bimboids, two or three young women groomed to covergirl standard with giggles like tinny cisterns.

They sat down as close to Boss as possible and laughed at his every second word. When Boss rose to go to the buffet to get his cornflakes, the Bimboids wheeched out handbag mirrors to check their lip-gloss, mascara and blusher. Promotion and favour depend on such things.

Last came Bitch, the toughened old broad, every wrinkle shouting hard living and hard playing; more of a Boy than all the Boys put together. The Tallulah Bankhead of British commerce. Trailing Gauloises fumes and stale scent. Seen It All, Done It All, Couldn't Give a Stuff.

Only Bitch caused the Armanis to pause. Only Bitch silenced the Bimboids and caused their pert little cheeks to clench. The PoPos slurped the last of their tea and stood up en masse. Wimps made their excuses and left. Boss studiously avoided her. Bitch was clearly a nasty bit of work.

Soon, Boss left, followed quickly by Bimboids and Armanis. Bitch was left to her fag, her politicking, her third cup of coffee and her thumping hangover.

And I, replete after one of the longest and most compelling breakfasts in years, retired bemused by the wheelings and dealings of British business and headed for the car park and open road, smiling.

This column won an award, although I forget exactly what. There's a plaque somewhere in one of the cupboards at home.

I think it appealed to the judges possibly because every office in Britain operates with Boss, Wimps, Bitch, Po-Pos, Armanis and Bimboids.

One of the puff delegates was an Aberdonian. I couldn't possibly say into which category he fell.

18. TOP-DRAWER TRAVEL

Or how to enjoy the company of a peer of the realm

████ ████ ████ ████

"No Telegraph and no Mail? What do you have on that cart of yours? Nothing of any interest to man nor beast, I suppose. Calcutta Bugle and Rat Breeder's Monthly?"

IT HAS been a panjandric week in the howe. I have had a brush with the aristocracy and, for just a moment, I sniffed how the other half lives. I neither sought it nor planned it; it just happened that way. One minute, I had taken my seat on an aircraft hoping, as all travellers do, that the seat next to me would remain empty so that I might have some half-decent elbow room; the next, there appeared at my side a chap of about 70 with a bearing that spoke of a military career.

He wore a pinstripe suit that once, many years before, had been Savile Row's finest, but which would have horrified its tailor now that it bore battle honours of several years' active service.

A slight stoop in the man's 6ft frame made him peer at me from beneath white, beetling brows, but his face was kindly and his manner beseeching and impeccably English as he inquired in a crystal accent if he could trouble me for access to his seat.

I stepped into the aisle. He manoeuvred in and almost fell back into his place with a pained sigh, then looked round at me and chortled heartily, perhaps at his own aches and stiffness.

"Awful weather," he said, sighing again and mopping a hankie across rain-soaked bleach-white hair, followed by a dicht and dab at an equally white moustache.

I might have taken him for a businessman, but the lack of a tie or briefcase or portable computer suggested not. He was certainly not a tourist, for tourists do not wear Savile Row suits to travel and, besides, what few tourists there were on the flight were all up at the back.

"Five hundred pounds," he said, staring into my face. "The ticket. Five hundred pounds for the ticket. A damned disgrace, wouldn't you say? Five hundred pounds?"

I said it was, but that I was fortunate that someone else was paying, otherwise I would have been flying up at the back, too.

"Five hundred pounds," he said, turning to stare out at the window, then turning back almost at once and adding: "I could fly to New York for that money and have a damned good holiday with the small change?"

I said I was sure he could.

"I'm glad to say someone else is paying for me, too," he said, "otherwise I should be in steerage like a shot. You meet a far nicer person in steerage, I think. They're all damned suits up here."

He gave a small, dismissive wave of his hand to emphasise his distaste of businesspeople. Clearly, he was not a businessman.

It was after several minutes of listening to the rhythms and cadences of his accent that I began to wonder if I was in top-drawer company. If you can imagine how the Prince of Wales will speak when he is in his 70s, toned with the slightly strangled, back-of-throat vowels of Malcolm Muggeridge, you have as accurate a description as I can give you.

When the stewardess came with a trolley of newspapers, he peered past me to see what was displayed. "Telegraph, my dear?" he inquired. She riffled through the titles, but could find none.

"Mail?" he said.

She could find no Mail, either.

"No Telegraph and no Mail?" he said. "You must have one of them, surely? They're quite common. What do you have on that little cart of yours? Nothing of any interest to man nor beast, I suppose. Calcutta Bugle and Rat Breeder's Monthly, is that it? Eh?"

In cold print, it looks brusque, but he said it with such warmth, and with such an impish grin that the stewardess could barely stifle her smile, and I was smiling hard into my lap myself. I was in the presence of an old charmer, and an aristocratic old charmer, at that.

"Well, well," he said. "No sale. No sale." She trundled off.

He turned to me. "No Telegraph and no Mail," he confided, as if I had not heard the conversation he had been conducting across my nose. He slumped back into his seat and sighed. "Five hundred quid and no Telegraph," he told himself sadly. "They'd better have a decent wine, that's all I can say."

Twenty minutes into the flight, I discovered that the wine was far from decent. At least, that was the considered opinion of my travelling companion, who had asked to be shown the selection of whites and looked utterly horrified as the stewardess held out two small bottles side by side so that he could peer across me at the labels.

"I could run my car on that," he said of the first bottle, so the stewardess pushed forward the second, which he studied even more closely. He looked up at her, a wicked glint in his eye. "Paint-strippah, my dear," he said quietly. "Paint-strippah."

He sat back in his seat while she apologised, then she wheeled her trolley farther back. "I'll wager you," he said to no one in particular, "that we get a disgusting hot meal shoved under our noses now, when it would be far better if airline companies would learn a basic lesson and serve decent cold food."

He sighed again. "Five hundred pounds, no Telegraph, no Mail, wine that would blister steel and warm swill for a meal. Travel certainly broadens the mind."

"And shrinks the wallet," I said, and he looked round at me and chortled.

"Do you know," he said, "a chum of mine has the right idea. He gets absolutely blotto — absolutely ratted — before a flight, falls asleep as soon as his behind hits the spot and, bless me, wakes up as his plane lands, sober as a judge. Marvellous trick, don't you think? Couldn't manage it myself. John Barleycorn doesn't agree with me. I learned that very early on and I've treated the devil with respect ever since."

The meal came and went. It was not British Airways at its best, but it was not as bad as my companion had feared, and perfectly edible. Presently, the liqueur trolley came round. I declined, and so did he. The stewardess was just about to trundle off when he changed his mind and called her back.

"I say," he said, "as you were. Would you have a small cognac about you?" She found him a miniature of brandy and presented him with it and a glass. "Thank you so much," he said warmly. "Very kind. Very kind."

She trundled off with her trolley and, from the corner of his eye, he watched her go, then quickly he slipped the miniature into his pocket and winked at me. "Five hundred quid," he said. "I'll be roaring tonight." He laughed that shoulder-wobbling laugh again.

"Do you know," he said, "I was in France a couple of weeks ago, driving back to England, so I decided to stop at one of those supermarkets near the Channel where it's frightfully cheap to stock up with beer." (He pronounced it *byah*.)

"I was just loading the last crate into the back of the estate car when I spotted someone I knew up to the same trick and he said: "Roland, what on earth are you intending to do with all that byah?'

"I looked at him and I said: 'My dear chap, if it's a hot day, I shall give a bottle to the gardener.' "

I still get people reminding me about "Calcutta Bugle and Rat Breeder's Monthly". All I can say is that the conversation happened exactly as you read it here, and although I might have been apprehensive at the start, Lord S********** turned out to be one of the most entertaining travelling companions it has been my good fortune to meet.

Would that they could all be so enervating.

19. CARELESS IN THE COMMUNITY

Or why hospital administrators don't always know best

━━ ━━ ━━ ━━

"These are extraordinary people with extraordinary needs,
and the overwhelming impression they make on anyone
who meets them is of their vulnerabilty."

IT HAS been a decretal week in the howe. On Sunday I was part of the judging panel for the sixth annual Festival of Music and Drama, organised by the staff of Woodlands Hospital, near Aberdeen.

They are kind enough to ask me back most years and I am pleased to attend because the enthusiasm and determination of the participants are infectious. It's a stony heart that doesn't leave the hall at the end of the day feeling cheered.

Woodlands staff organise the festival, but it draws its talent from much farther afield. Four other establishments for mentally handicapped people throughout Grampian and Tayside send great busloads of residents and helpers every year. How order comes from such chaos is a marvel of logistics.

This year, the joy was just as infectious. An outsider would have seen the brightly painted props and sets, and the residents showing off their costumes proudly and would have noticed little difference.

Yet there was a poignancy to this year's event. The threat of closure hangs over Woodlands. In April, it might well shut for good. The same fate awaits Kingseat Hospital and Arduthie Hospital, Stonehaven.

The residents are unaware of what hangs over them, of course; they were too intent on doing their best for their festival. And the staff put up their usual sterling show on Sunday without complaint or politics, but the closure plan was uppermost in the minds of the parents and friends sitting at the back in the shadows.

In the name of fiscal efficiency, and a Government target drawn up somewhere in the Department of Health, Woodlands residents will be decanted from their home, and the security of the staff they cling to as friends.

Some will be put into Care in the Community schemes. Others will be rehoused in a purpose-built unit in the grounds of an Aberdeen mental hospital, which demonstrates a wilful oversight of the yawning chasm between mental handicap and mental illness.

Whether or not Care in the Community is appropriate for those Woodlands people earmarked for it is open to debate. The Government, the trusts and senior policy staff who are more obsessed with following policy than listening to families' wishes make great play of giving people with a mental disability "the right to lead an ordinary life in ordinary circumstances" and reflecting "everyone's right to live within the community".

The flaw here is that these are quite patently not ordinary lives in ordinary circumstances. Anyone who contends that they are is a fool.

These are extraordinary people with extraordinary needs, and the overwhelming impression they make on anyone who meets them is of their vulnerabilty. It is that vulnerability, and their loving and trusting natures, which so many people throughout Grampian feel is being exploited. I suspect that within a couple of years Care in the Community will be seen as Careless in the Community. I hope I am proved wrong.

The drive to efficiency is an unfeeling master. While no one approves of profligacy in a public body, and everyone understands the need to get the most bang for your buck, as Americans would say, that cannot be done independently of human feeling, and it is those feelings — of people who will be entirely bewildered by what will be done to them — that will be manoeuvred and shunted and damaged if the closure plan is approved. Knowing how open these people are emotionally; how trusting and loving and joyous and vulnerable they are, I wouldn't want to have their hurt on my conscience.

These views are my own. They might or might not coincide with anyone else's; parents, residents or staff. But I should stress here that no member of Woodlands staff has spoken to me about the threat of closure or said anything in any way critical of their employers.

I mention that only because so many employees of hospital trusts — specifically Grampian Healthcare NHS Trust and Aberdeen Royal Hospitals NHS Trust — seem to fear retribution if they speak out at what is being done in the name of the bottom line.

How do we know this? We know because of the number of letters, filled with despair and anger, which we receive weekly from all branches of hospital staff throughout the Press and Journal circulation area.

From consultants to nursing staff to cleaners, they ask that their names and addresses are withheld if we print their views because they fear for their futures if they are seen to be critical of the new regimes.

It says a great deal about trust managements if staff are so fearful that the only way they feel able to express an opinion safely is behind a veil of anonymity in a newspaper. It says just as much for their courage and their dedication to what they believe is right that they are prepared to take that risk.

Such a fundamental fault in the way an organisation is perceived by its staff is something that it needs to address long before it scrambles for Government targets. If any organisation finds that its people are not behind it, cannot trust it or fear it, it is derelict in its duty already. If the foundation is weak, there is little point in doing any building.

Staff attitudes might not particularly concern hospital trusts, of course. I suspect they do not. We know already that the Grampian trust sets very little store by the views of parents. Its chief executive's outburst seven weeks ago dismissing parental concerns as "hysterical" and the work of "mischief-makers" says everything we need to know about the trust's management, interpersonal and communication skills.

And if trust management are so dismissive of the opinions of parents, friends and staff, can they really expect us to be convinced by their repeated assertion that the best interests of the residents are their priority while they drive to save the next couple of million?

The residents are their easiest target, after all. They trust and love everyone.

And they don't speak back.

━━ ━━ ━━ ━━

You can imagine that this 1994 column didn't go down well at the health trust concerned. That was unfortunate, but not particularly worrying.

The outcome was bizarre, however. The part that really rattled them was the contention that health-service staff in the North-east were too frightened of being victimised to speak out.

A senior trust officer called to dispute, very amiably, the notion that senior figures at the trust ruled autocratically or that staff feared for their jobs. "We have an active staff-relations council as a forum for them to express their views," he said.

Then came the good bit. "How about if I got someone on the council to write in to point out that they have complete freedom to say what they feel?" he asked. "Would you publish it?"

He did and, loving the irony, we did publish.

20. FLIGHTS OF FANCIES

Or how to spot a first-class tearoom without going inside

■■■ ■■ ■■ ■■

"A proper, old-fashioned tearoom; one with teapots and
hot-water jugs and a tiered plate of caramel squares,
battenburg and other fancy pieces."

IT HAS been a cibarious week in the howe. Periodically, and on the pretext of getting out of the house to enjoy a sunny weekend afternoon, I persuade the CO to tumble into the car and we go off bowling along the highways and by-ways of the North-east.

I enjoy these afternoons especially because our destinations are towns that, nowadays, too many people know only as words on road-signs. Tens of thousands of drivers hammer past the likes of Huntly, Stonehaven and Forres every week, forgetting the delights waiting just a few hundred yards off the by-pass, so the CO and I have made it our business to remind ourselves whenever we can that our part of Scotland is not just a network of tarry strips and commuters.

I say "pretext" of getting out of the house because while the CO looks forward to a change of loaf, a different museum and a rake around new shops, I am nursing my ulterior motive.

I am there because I know that, eventually, she will say: "I fancy a coffee. What about you?"

This means that we are about to step into a tearoom; a proper, old-fashioned tearoom; one with teapots and hot-water jugs and a tiered plate of caramel squares, battenburg and other fancy pieces.

We favour the tearooms that are obviously family-run, the two clues being, first, a peer through the window to see if the place is swarming with pensioners. That's good. Pensioners can sniff out a first-rate tearoom quicker than bloodhounds find an escaped convict.

The second clue, the clincher, is a big sign in the window reading:

Home Bakes

Find such a tearoom and your afternoon fly is transformed from just a hurried stop to fill a holie. It becomes a wallow in the very essence of the North-east — because you can eavesdrop.

I lug into other people's conversations and do so without shame.

It is my only vice.

Honest.

Eavesdroppers rarely patronise chain cafés. Even the good ones are pretty faceless and, maybe you've noticed, the clientele always seems to be chewing sadly, like cattle on valium. If not chewing, they are staring silently at what they have bought or gazing out of the window as if they are unable to comprehend their foolishness and are dreaming of escape.

There's certainly not much conversation, illicit or otherwise, so chain cafés don't offer much in the way of the local colour which eavesdroppers need. The establishments to avoid, in my experience, are the ones with a small bottle of tomato ketchup and a plastic carnation on each table.

Happily, we had found a likely tearoom at a prominent North-east town at the weekend. It passed the pensioner test and the home-bakes rule, and was especially promising because as we opened the door to enter, a silence fell over the place.

As any eavesdropper knows, this is hitting the jackpot. It means that all manner of scandal is being discussed and has been put on hold until the assembly establishes whether or not the new arrivals are strangers and thus safe, or, if local, are to be trusted.

Pensioners stopped in mid-chew of their macaroons. Cups halted mid-way between saucers and lips as the patrons surveyed the new arrivals as discreetly as they could. If we caught the gaze of any, they looked away quickly, as if they had been only admiring the curtains or filling in time by looking idly for cobwebs.

We were directed to a table in the corner. Once we settled ourselves, the buzz of conversation began again, gently at first, then soon back to full volume.

Almost at once, I heard float across the room:

". . . in aneth the bed. Dizzens o them."

To the inquisitive soul of a writer, snippets such as that are the very breath.

Dozens of what? Cockroaches? Magazines? Forgotten pos?

Alas, I can't tell you, for the waitress arrived at our table. She was a fresh-faced young thing, obviously still at the town academy, but with a Saturday job to finance her make-up.

And this is the other marvellous thing about North-east tearooms. Waitresses don't leer at you and ask in some faux-Surrey accent: "How may I help you?"

This is because any North or North-east waitress tends to understand that, as she works in a café, it is pretty obvious how she may help you.

Our waitress paused by the side of our table, pencil poised above her pad, tongue pressed doggedly out of the side of her mouth to aid concentration, and said simply: "Aye?"

It was just like home.

And if you'll excuse me going off at a tangent, we were once in a café at Fraserburgh when the young waitress came across and, in a Buchan drawl so broad I could have kissed her, said with great courtesy: "And fit are ye sikkin?"

Back to the eavesdropping. It became apparent fairly quickly that an elderly couple two tables away were to be the likeliest sources.

Their Doric was broad and the conversation a little louder than most, perhaps because after a lifetime of working a tractor (I took the bunnet at the side of the table, the tweed jacket, the impeccable brown brogues and the ruddy complexion to be marks of a retired farmer) he had been made a little deaf and didn't realise quite how loudly he was speaking.

If you are that couple, I apologise now, but you made my afternoon.

They were discussing the impending arrival of a baby in their home village, and it became clear that the mother-to-be was unmarried.

The woman said little. When she spoke at all, it was in clipped, short sentences that I couldn't quite make out. She was clearly disapproving; one of the old school who had no time for modern social mores. She knew what was right. She knew what was proper, and unmarried mothers were clearly neither right nor proper.

The husband, on the other hand, had that cheery, easy manner of a chap who has seen a lot in life and for whom nothing was much of a scandal any more.

On several occasions, he admonished his wife with a long, drawling: "Na, na, na."

But it was when he leaned back as their conversation drew to a close that he came out with an old country saying that I hadn't heard spoken for years.

"Fitivver," he said, dismissing her arguments with a wave of his hand. "A bick's aye the better o a pup.' "

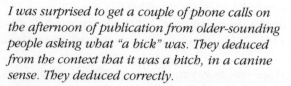

I was surprised to get a couple of phone calls on the afternoon of publication from older-sounding people asking what "a bick" was. They deduced from the context that it was a bitch, in a canine sense. They deduced correctly.

This time, I'm not prepared to reveal where the tearoom in question was. Your only clue is that it was quite near a ruined castle.

21. A QUESTION OF BREEDING

Or how to pick yourself a four-legged friend

"I had barely sat down on his sofa when one of the dogs stood up, loped across to me, rested his head in my lap and looked up with the most trusting eyes. That was it."

IT HAS been a theriological week in the howe. We acquired a new member of the family during the summer holiday, and I have discovered the first truths of parenthood: solitude is a luxury and quiet lies beyond the bounds of human hope.

We have bought a puppy.

Like all babies, he has difficulty with bowel control and has little concept of night and day. Fundamentally, he eats, sleeps, howls, scratches, poos, piddles, blows off and, frankly, does very little else of any earthly use. Just like a husband, says Mrs Harper.

For the moment, the deal seems a bit one-sided. We ply him with Puppy Supreme, Weetabix and milk. We speak to him, cuddle him, play with him, show him round the policies and provide secure and cosy accommodation.

In return, he looks up at us with languid puppy eyes and keechs all over the laundry floor. Sometimes, we turn up first thing in the morning and wonder how so much could have come from so little — and whether or not he has been revolving at high speed on the end of a rope while doing so.

We endure it in the earnest hope that he will become a more entertaining companion as he grows a little older. For the moment, it is a battle of wills and Jeyes Fluid.

I have not owned a dog before, although I have long wanted to. Dogs and I have had an understanding since my childhood weekends on my aunt and uncle's farm, when Flossie, their collie cross, and I would go exploring.

The memories of those days, probably tinted more rosy with every passing year, only bolster my belief that every small boy should have a dog. There is no truer companion for any human, but especially so for a child. To an eight-year-old, a dog's welcome is exhilarating because it is unconditional love and unbounded enthusiasm. A dog treated properly will offer friendship at its purest. A dog will never fall out with you. A dog will never sulk. A dog will never pinch your train set.

Small wonder that American psychologists prescribe dogs for the dejected, and who could have demurred when a Manchester University study declared recently that stress levels of dog-owners and cat-owners are up to 20% lower than those of the petless? It's something to do with strokes, pats and bosies.

Much as I love dogs, I couldn't have contemplated owning one until now. While I lived in Aberdeen for six years in the 1980s, leaving a dog along in a flat for 12 hours a day would have been unfair at best and cruel at worst. Only when I moved back to the arms of the howe did the notion occur again.

But which breed?

I found quickly that there was very little point in talking to other dog-owners; every master thinks his dog is the pinnacle of canine perfection. Every dog's old man believes that contemplating any other breed is madness and irresponsibility.

So the keeshond-owner insisted that a keeshond was essential because it didn't cast and was placid and affectionate. The alsatian's owner insisted that it was loyal and had had a wholly bad press for no reason at all. The boxer's owner said it had character and was easily trained. The labrador's owner said that if so many blind people relied on labs for guidance, the breed was irreproachably stable and intelligent.

For months, we mulled over almost 200 different breeds. Some were too aggressive. Some were so overbred in all the wrong directions that they had become cruel caricatures. Some were impractically small and some impractically large. Some were prone to character flaws and some so laid back that they might as well have been cushions.

We didn't want a lifestyle dog. We didn't want to buy a dog in the same way that some people buy a car — to affect a pose. We certainly didn't want to buy a dog at Christmas for, knowing what we know now, only a complete neep would buy a dog at the end of the year, and only a bigger neep would sell him one.

A year ago, we had whittled it down to a shortlist of two. Both had long lists of advantages, but one breed, allegedly, was daft as a brush and completely untrainable. The other was sullen and, according to the book, needed up to 10 miles of exercise a day.

We were still swithering when, one Saturday evening in the summer, we visited a neighbour who owned a pair of one of our shortlisted breeds. I had barely sat down on his sofa when one of the dogs stood up in the corner, loped across to me, rested his head in my lap and looked up with the most trusting eyes.

And that was it. That was the hook moment. If we were to get a dog at all, it would be an Irish Setter.

We researched the breed periodically. You don't rush into buying a dog; the last things you want are surprises. I spoke to some of the North-east's most respected doggy experts, vets and trainers. We found out about diseases, care, temperament, breed lines and likely 10-year care costs.

And a few days ago we called the pre-eminent breeder of Irish in North Scotland, Pat Dempster, and asked if we could visit. "We just want to chat," I said. "We're not ready to buy yet. I think we know all the positives, but we want to know the negatives, too."

So we turned up at Pat's farm one afternoon and we had a two-hour chat in the lounge. Just before we were due to leave for the final deliberations, we asked if we could see some puppies. Five minutes later, a mum and three bundles of russet were on the carpet nuzzling our feet. An hour later, we were bound for the howe with a cardboard box and a small occupant.

It's early days yet. He didn't take to unfamiliar surroundings and began howling at 3.30am on his first night. We're improving all the time, though. We expect to get a full night's sleep some time around the middle of September. Until then, I am ploughing through the dog-psychology books, ready for the day later this year when formal training begins. We have learned already that it was a mistake to give him an old towel for play, and that sleeping must be allowed only in his basket, not around feet.

Meanwhile, if anyone can tell me how to get him to evacuate every time in the same part of the garden, and not all over the place like scatter-bombs, I'll be only too glad to hear from you.

Which left us only a name to choose. We wanted something literary, or red, or Irish, but nothing seemed to fit. Instead, it came to us in a moment of inspiration.

We have called him Stronach.

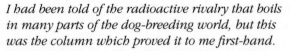

I had been told of the radioactive rivalry that boils in many parts of the dog-breeding world, but this was the column which proved it to me first-hand.

I had a letter from a dreadful old trout; one of those busybodies who thinks that because your name appears in public you have to thole any old nonsense she cares to dish up.

She presumed, in the most offensive terms, to know everything about how we were keeping the puppy; the manner in which we had bought him; what we were feeding him, and what books I had read.

Since I have never put up with nonsense, she was sent off, to her great surprise and outrage, with a metaphorical clap in the lugs, her backside in flames and told to mind her own business.

Stronach is now five, doing exceptionally well and possessed of a boundless enthusiasm that I envy.

22. COMRADES AND CUCUMBERS

Or why salads turn up where you least expect them

■■■ ■■■ ■■■ ■■■

"Temperatures plunged to -20C in the Arctic night.
Only once have I been in a place colder than Murmansk,
and that was Braemar one April local holiday."

IT HAS been an incandescent week in the howe. I am
recovering from an assignment to Murmansk, that pearl of the
Russian north coast. Intriguing though it was, it is reassuring
to be back in a mixed economy. "And what was it like?" everyone
keeps asking. Well, it was cold. Cold is what it was. Cold and
snowy. Snowy and dark. And ice. A lot of ice.

So much snow and ice there was that when I asked to be taken
to the cemetery for British sailors who perished in the Arctic
convoys during the Great Patriotic War (1941-45), they took me to
a field of snow and told me that the first gravestone started four
feet below where I was standing and was due to make its annual
debut around the third week of May.

Surprisingly, there were no snowploughs in the city, or none
that I saw, but at three every morning a lorry drove up and down
the street outside my hotel with a circular saw spinning at its
flanks and cut blocks of ice from the sides of the streets. No, I'm
not joking.

Temperatures soared to -7C at midday and plunged to -20C in
the depths of the Arctic night.

Only once have I been in a place colder than Murmansk, and
that was Braemar one April local holiday.

The compensation for these sub-human temperatures was a hospitality which burned so fiercely that you'd have been forgiven for wondering if they were all high on something.

For a nation undergoing such rigours and strictures in travelling the road to a free-market economy, Russians set great store by entertaining a visitor properly and by sharing what little they have. The vigour with which they set about making sure their visitor from Scotland was treated royally was touching and, frankly, humbling. I hope we treat them even half as well.

And although communism has crumbled, patriotism has not. The Russian flag flies at seemingly every third building. From old soldiers to small children, all declaim loudly that they are Russian, have always been Russian and will always be Russian, no matter what historical hiccups they have endured, and what privations are spread before them.

Tenacity and stoicism are words writ large in the modern Russian vocabulary.

As is cucumber.

Food in this far-flung outpost is better than Western tastes expect, but they do have this tedious obsession with the long, green, watery vegetable. Should merciful fate decree that cucumbers and I will not confront each other again until a week after the end of eternity, it will still be a month too soon.

Sliced cucumber, diced cucumber and riced cucumber. Cucumber soup. Cucumber salad. Cucumber with fried egg. Cucumber with potato salad. Cucumber, fried egg and potato salad.

Where they get them, heaven knows, but a fortune awaits the first person who compiles the definitive cookbook 101 Ways with Cucumbers and has it translated into Russian for the export market.

No cucumbers, however, on board the icebreaker Yamal, a ship built in 1989 which roves the Arctic Ocean keeping trading and fishing routes open and, by good fortune, happened to be in dock for a two-week refit during my stay.

I was taken to meet the captain, a doughty fellow of good humour, 50-odd summers, greying hair and faltering English.

His first words were: "You wish tour of ship?" Who would be so unadventurous as to decline the offer of a VIP tour round the pride of the Russian civil fleet, in the company of one of most senior naval officers of the old Soviet Union?

Not I.

As he ushered me up and down ladders, along gangways and around the deck, I couldn't help musing that, only five years before, the notion of showing a Western writer round the vanguard of Russian naval technology would have been unthinkable. Yet here I was, given free access to anything and everything.

"Yes, of course you may see communications room."

"Please join me on bridge."

"Take photographs."

"You like?"

I liked very much. I liked it even more when, after an hour or two, and he had clearly decided that I rated minimally on the international scale of potential subversives, he leaned over our coffee and whispered: "I wish to show you something."

I leaned over to him. "You do?"

He nodded and stood up, beckoning me to follow him back into the intimmers of his ship. Down we went. Down and down. Down and down and down. The ladders getting ever steeper and even narrower. The decor growing ever more utilitarian.

Then, with my knees beginning to ache, we broke out into a small room, lit by a single 40-watt bulb, where the heat was intense, the air stale and the smell of fresh paint hung heavily.

He pointed to a small oven-sized door in an otherwise plain steel wall. His look urged me to open it. So I opened it. And there was a sheet of thick glass.

I peered through. Above me, to both sides and away below, was a vast cavern not unlike a James Bond film set. Little men in red overalls clambered over turbines and driveshafts, pipes and tubes.

I turned back to the captain, clearly not looking sufficiently impressed, for he pointed me back to the aperture, insisting that I study the two large metal cases which sat quietly in the depths of this most prodigious chamber.

So I did. And I looked back at him, nodding sagely, but with not a clue if I should look impressed or knowledgeable or what.

"Nuclear reactors," he said, beaming.

I closed that oven door with, I hope, not unseeming haste, and led the way up and out of the ship's heart two steps at a time. I would have been on top of the radar gantry had not the captain caught up with me and diverted me back to his lounge to finish our coffee.

He slapped my back and grinned as he assured me that the heart of his ship was safer than being outside in natural background radiation.

"Very safe." he said nodding. "Very, very safe."

Aye, right enough.

So I am back in the howe, suffering no apparent ill-effects after my unwitting brush with the atomic age, apart from a heavy bout of flu and a profound aversion to all things cucumiform.

But if you happen to be driving through the howe in the wee sma oors and you see a shimmering, ghostly green glow at the north end, don't panic; it's nothing supernatural or extra-terrestrial.

It's only me up for a drink of water.

▬ ▬ ▬ ▬

Visiting Murmansk has been one of the great experiences of my time at the Press and Journal, although I have often pondered the fact that other people are sent on assignment to the Caribbean, Kenya, Italy and the USA, while I get the Russian Arctic in March, Israel's West Bank in January and Dundee.

A more paranoid person might begin to worry.

23. LATE NIGHT AT THE SUPERMARKET

Or how our masters could learn lessons in the aisles

▬ ▬ ▬ ▬

"There was a pride about her bearing. She was certainly not a down-and-out. It seemed she had simply fallen on hard times and had had to resolve to make the best of it."

IT HAS been an emporiate week in the howe. We had intended to round off our last week's holiday of 1993 by sharing in the national resurgence of cinemagoing. One of my special treats as a small boy was being allowed to stay up in my dressing-gown to see David Janssen evade the law as he tried to track down the one-armed man. How well would Harrison Ford stand comparison in the 1990s cinema version of The Fugitive?

And the answer is . . . I can't tell you.

With this family's customary forward planning, we had not planned on such a globally blockbusting movie being relegated already to Cinema Two. Consequently, we stood in a queue in a howling, rainy gale outside the cinema for 10 minutes on Friday night when a man in a bow tie appeared and told us that all the available seats had bottoms in them.

A trio of young blades at the front, in jeans and Doctor Marten's boots seemed considerably put out. "Oh, come, good fellow," quoth they. "Surely you jest, for we have been arraigned in such inclement weather. Can you not find it in your heart to permit us entry, failing which your personal safety might be the subject of discussion?" Or words to that effect.

As my wife and I tripped through puddles under a shared

umbrella on the way back to the car, we took consolation in the knowledge that, while that notorious Aberdeen Harbour wind had geiled us to the bone, the cinema industry was basking in the balmy breeze of renewed business and burgeoning optimism.

However, I grudge the petrol to travel all the way into Aberdeen only to travel all the way out again. This has nothing to do with being environmentally friendly and everything to do with Aberdeenshire blood. I had to justify the journey.

So we went shopping.We drove to the nearest thing Aberdeen has to an all-night superstore and parked in its almost-deserted car park. Half-past eight on a Friday night is an odd time to be in a superstore. Unless you work in a supermarket, you're likely unaware of the change of character which visits your friendly neighbourhood megamultiple in that last half-hour of business before 9pm. It's quite mesmerising.

For a start, employees outnumber the shoppers. Fresh-produce staff survey what is left unsold in the display cabinets and congratulate each other on judging the day's salad stuffs quite well, although "that amount o watercress is disappintin".

Younger male staff humph crates of apples and whizz round corners with ranks of trolleys, clattering into boxes of dates, swapping stories of their recent social lives and practising incisive character critique of whichever colleague happens to have the night off.

But the shoppers at that time of night are even more interesting. At a good guess, there were not more than a dozen. There were a few singles (probably students), a couple of middle-aged men of indeterminate sobriety looking for a cheap deal on cans of export, an exasperated young husband, wife and child, a trio in from the country, ourselves . . . and then I spotted her.

As chief trolley-pusher and deputy comestible-gatherer, I was standing guard over our trolley, idly wondering whether what patak is and whether or not there really is a demand from North-east households for such avant-garde cuisine.

"Fit did ye hae for yer tea last nicht, Wullie?"

"A pun o' patak and a softie and syrup."

"Oh, what fine. We'd cheese and breid wirsels."

Anyway, there was I wondering, when a trolley hove in sight at the end of the aisle. It hovered for a few seconds, then continued, and into view came a small, bent old figure in a heavy brown coat.

She peered out from under a teacosy hat and struggled manfully with a trolley which refused to change direction until, with much puffing and grunting, she persuaded it down the aisle in which I was stationed.

She was already halfway round the store, but her trolley carried virtually nothing. Even a hand-basket would have looked ridiculously unfilled with that amount of groceries. As she walked slowly towards me, eyes intent on the brightly lit shelves, I could see that her coat was past its best. Her shoes, too, were done and certainly couldn't have kept out the wet.

Her face was ruddy and lined; her cheeks rosy with the cold; her eyes watery. She stopped to pick out a jar of something and studied it, then she put it back and carried on past me. Her trolley had two apples, something from the meat counter with a yellow sticker on it which meant presumably that it had been reduced for a quick sale, a small tin of dog food, a small tin of beans and a leek.

From behind, the coat was covered in dog hairs and the thick stockings were laddered in two or three places, and I couldn't help but study her as she wandered away from me. She was quite oblivious. But there was a pride about her bearing. She was certainly not a down-and-out. It seemed she had simply fallen on hard times and had had to resolve to make the best of it.

Just then, the young couple with the toddler turned into the bottom of the aisle. As the old lady approached them, she caught the eye of the toddler in the trolley seat and went across to say something to the child and smile a friendly smile. The young couple pushed past her, not even acknowledging her existence, and the old woman watched as the child was propelled away.

My heart sank. A gesture of kindness being rebuffed so coldly must have hurt an old lady.

But she carried on round the bottom of the aisle and disappeared, studying more jars and packets and tins that she probably couldn't afford.

I didn't see her again for another 15 minutes. While we were checking out at one till, she was two tills farther along, and there seemed to be some discussion between herself and the checkout operator. She was raking through her eight or 10 items and picked out what looked like the tin of dog food.

"It's all right," said the young lad on the till, "we'll put it back later."

"I took it," she said, "and I'll put it back."

While she walked off to replace an item which, I can only presume, had broken her budget, the young lad at the till caught my gaze and shrugged his shoulders. For a moment, I wanted to go across and pay the difference for her. I wrestled with myself for too long about the conflicting merits of her self-respect and her need, for she was soon back, collected her groceries and change and shuffled off.

The really sad thing about this woman is not that she is old, or lonely, or on so tight a budget that a tin of dog food breaks the bank.

The really sad thing is that she's not the only one.

Last thing on a Friday at the supermarket would be a telling lesson for many a politician.

▬ ▬ ▬ ▬

One letter after this column appeared berated me gently for not paying for all the woman's groceries, which was a fine sentiment except that you can't intrude on people's self-respect by barging in and offering to buy their messages for them.

Besides, had you seen this woman, you'd have known that, poor as she was, she would have been grossly offended.

24. BOORISHNESS AT 35,000ft

Or how tempting it is to clap an arrogant businessman in the lugs

▬ ▬ ▬ ▬

"He wanted to impress the cabin crew that he was a man
not to be tangled with. He was a man who counted.
He was a man who got things done."

✺

IT HAS been a coxcombical week in the howe. I was involved
in an air drama 40 feet over the runway on the final approach
to landing at Aberdeen Airport.

If the day concluded with a drama, it hadn't been much better at
the start. I had been in London. London is stressful even on a
spring Sunday morning, but last Thursday was a real humdinger.
A 4.30am start and half a dozen different meetings, interviews and
delays do little for the digestion and demeanour.

By the time I flopped into my aisle seat on the British Airways
737, due to take off for Aberdeen at 19.25, I was not in the finest
of fine fettle; I'll admit that now. I sat down, pushed my hand
baggage under the seat in front and pulled out the Scott Turow
novel I had been reading.

When I have been given an aisle seat and I have boarded early,
I never fasten the seat belt straight away. Usually, someone
boarding later will want access to their seat by the window or in
the middle of the row of three. So there I sat, reading quietly,
while the 76 other passengers trooped aboard. I was in the middle
of a particularly gripping scene (the hero had just found a body in
his chum's fridge) when a newspaper shot past my nose — so
close that I could have read the fish prices — and landed in the

seat by the window. From the corner of my eye I could see a three-piece suit stuffing his Burberry and briefcase into the overhead locker. A businessman. Mid-40s. Greying, receding hair. Sallow complexion. Incipient pot belly from too many business-lunch roly-polys and custard. And an attitude. One of those businessmen.

You might be happy about strangers flinging newspapers across the front of your face, but it doesn't inspire me over much. Not after a flat-out 14-hour day. Not as a mark of courtesy.

He finished packing away his chattels then simply stood in the aisle beside me. I waited for the: "Excuse me, please", but it didn't come. I waited for: "Could I squeeze past into my seat?", but no. Just silence. I was meant to snap to attention and hop out of my seat.

So I'm afraid I just let him stand there. And I decided that he would stand there until he could bring himself to say something. I carried on reading.

So he stood there. And I sat there. And he stood there. And I sat there. And he sighed pointedly, and his sigh was a mark that here was a very important fellow, not used to being kept waiting.

So he was kept waiting.

He cleared his throat. I looked up. The glower said: "Are you insolent or just stupid?" I was about to go back to my reading when it spoke. It pointed and it said: "That's my seat."

Thirty years of memories swirled before me and I could hear, away back in the early 1960s, my grandmother remonstrating with me when I pouted and pointed at the things I wanted and stamped my little feet.

So I looked up at him and, quoting her verbatim, said: "And what is the magic word?"

With very bad grace, from clenched teeth came a strangled: "Could - I - get - to - my - seat, - *please?*"

So I stood up, and ushered him through. Courtesy can be quite painless, really.

I found myself wondering if he was the sort of middle-aged man who blusters and puffs at dinner parties about the dreadful manners and boorishness of today's teenagers. I suspect he was.

The flight itself was uneventful, although the pilot warned us of very windy conditions ahead at Aberdeen. How right he was. If you read last Friday's Press and Journal, you know that the last flight up from Gatwick suffered all manner of calamities. That was my flight.

The pilot descended perfectly smoothly, considering how the 737 was being buffeted. At about, oh, 40ft over the runway, with the wings waggling up and down and the whole fuselage yawing as he struggled to keep it controlled, a particularly lusty gust blew us off line.

So he opened up the throttles again and, very smoothly, we climbed away from Aberdeen Airport. No drama. No screams. No luggage tumbling from the overhead lockers. No Charlton Heston striding up the aisle. No call to International Rescue.

We levelled out at 15,000ft. and the pilot explained that we would have to divert to Edinburgh, where weather conditions were calmer.

We landed at Edinburgh and taxied to an off-stand halt. And we waited. The pilot came on the intercom again to explain that the Met Office has said that the storm in Aberdeen was the result of a very low depression sitting over the city, but the depression had been very fast-moving and that, even now, wind conditions were settling. We were refuelling and would get another weather report in 10 minutes just to confirm that the Aberdeen storm had passed.

At around 10pm, the intercom hummed again. The windstorm had passed but, unfortunately, by the time we would be on final approach to Aberdeen, the airport would have shut. Consequently, we were stuck in Edinburgh and two coaches were being arranged to drive us north. We would arrive at about 2am. Sorry.

There was much groaning, as you can imagine, but my fellow-travellers and I took it in comparatively good part. There was little option. Just one of life's little adventures.

All except my travelling companion. He demanded a complaint form. And he wanted it *now*.

I have spent a great deal of time since last Thursday wondering what he wrote on his British Airways complaints form. He can't have complained about British Airways, for they were impeccably courteous throughout, and I would far rather have diverted to Edinburgh than crashed at Aberdeen.

He can't have complained about BAA, which runs Aberdeen Airport, because they don't decide what time the airport shuts.

He can't have complained about Aberdeen District Council, which fixes the shutdown time, because it was a British Airways complaints form, after all, and the sensible thing would have been to complain to the council if he felt so strongly.

So I have come to the conclusion that he must have been complaining about the real villain of the piece — the wind.

I can't get out of my mind a picture of him standing on the tarmac, shaking his fist furiously at the sky and shouting: "You naughty, naughty wind!"

The truth, of course, is that he wanted to impress the cabin crew that he was a man not to be tangled with. He was a man who counted. He was a man who got things done. He was a man who carried a real-leather briefcase and spoke in figures. He was a man who didn't stand any nonsense except his own.

He was a puffed-up, gold-seal, 24-carat prat.

▬ ▬ ▬ ▬

A pilot wrote to thank The Press and Journal for highlighting the boorish behaviour of some passengers. We published his letter, and I'm afraid the story was picked up by the tabloids. It drew him all manner of sanctimonious criticism from fellow-pilots and businesspeople who were appalled that anyone could think a fare-paying passenger was anything other than a minor deity.

But I know he was right. Good on you, sir.

25. FACE LIKE A SAFT TATTIE

Or the unspoken truth about every baby ever born

▬ ▬ ▬ ▬

"I'm sorry to say that the breath caught in my throat.
Inside lay the most astonishingly ugly baby it has been my
misfortune to meet."

I T HAS been a dendronic week in the howe. Now that our array of tubed-trees is well-established, even thriving, we have been seized by a notion for a collection of fruit trees in a small area at the back.

I say we had the notion, but it was the CO who hatched the plan. We had gone out to patrol the policies one evening after Easter when she had paused to gaze into the middle distance.

Seasoned husbands know to be wary of such gazes because of their propensity to lead to hard physical labour, but I walked forward to stand next to her and peer in the same direction.

All I could see was half an acre of old tree stumps, last winter's dead grass and a few clumps of dead reeds where the ground is heavy and low-lying, all enclosed on three fronts by broom that had grown too spindly to serve any useful purpose.

The CO, however, was seeing The Garden of Eden. Before her spread a lush lawn. Apple and cherry blossom fluttered on balmy southern breezes while a marble fountain tinkled in the background. The two of us were sitting on either side of a flower-twined garden swing, idly sipping Pimms, clad entirely in white and looking like a shampoo commercial.

Work to turn reality into this wild fantasy began last weekend with the first three apple trees, a spade, a bucket and a pick. Since the ground has never been cultivated, I and my back now know what superhuman effort our forebears put into making northern Scotland plenteous.

With rootstock, spurs, leaders and other such fructiferous terms swirling in my head, I barely heard the car drawing up at the end of the drive. Pausing only to draw the back of my hand across a sweat-stained brow and to peer through the broom, I spotted a vehicle that was not familiar to me.

As far as I was aware, we knew nobody owning that model, and not even as it drew closer and disappeared behind the far side of the house could I identify the solitary occupant.

I finished planting the second tree, making sure that it lined up with the first and that it was well-watered in before debating whether or not to return to base and the company of a stranger, or to continue as Johnny Appleseed.

Never the most social creature, the arrival of visitors is normally my cue to clear off. However the labour of howking unbroken ground using little more than a pick and spade is a marvellous incentive to brave the company of strangers, and I shambled back to the house.

There, I was introduced to Felicity (not her real name), a chum from the CO's early teaching days who had arrived from her new home in the English West Midlands on a brief holiday and had tracked us down."

In the CO's bosie, being rocked gently back and forth, was a bundle of rags that was clearly the real purpose of the visit. Felicity had come to show the CO her new baby.

Since Felicity and her issue are now safely back in the English West Midlands, I can be candid once more and declare that I am not a baby enthusiast, and that nothing I saw on Sunday made me change my beliefs.

Babies serve no useful purpose, cannot converse, be bidden or make their own brose. They represent work when most of us are already labouring under a surfeit of it. When a baby is not howling and keeping everyone awake, it makes odours so sour, putrid and thick you could knit cardigans.

"Look, Norman," said the CO. "Felicity's had a baby. His name's Matthew. Hello, Matthew. Hello, Matthew. Are you a good boy?"

"Congratulations," I said. "How old?"

"Two months," said Felicity. "Seven pounds, thirteen ounces."

I was about to observe that that must have been sore when the CO said: "Come and see." Against my better judgment, I approached and, as I approached, the CO asked: "Could Norman have a shottie?"

She made the query knowing perfectly well that I would no more like "a shottie" of a baby than I would want to go through the disembowelling machine at a chicken factory.

"What a shame," I said. "I've been planting trees and I'm absolutely filthy. Maybe next time."

She held out the bundle for me to see and I duly peeped in, preparing to make all the right noises. I'm sorry to say that the breath caught in my throat. Inside lay the most astonishingly ugly baby it has been my misfortune to meet.

A bappit nose, puffy cheeks, beady eyes and a skite of frizzy hair like a torn lavvie brush meant that it had no redeeming features whatsoever.

I could tell from the fixed smile on the CO's face that she was struggling with much the same opinion and was looking for a way out without telling lies and without hurting her friend's feelings.

Felicity, blinded by maternal hormones, was clearly unaware that she had given birth to a clootie dumpling.

"My," I said, trying to hit the right note of empathy, sympathy and wonder. "What a . . . character."

The CO sensed my dilemma and tried to find a way out by saying: "I've been trying to decide who he's most like."

Had I been truthful, I would have said: "W.C. Fields on a Friday-night bender."

"People say that he's got his father's eyes," said Felicity, gently pulling back the lambswool blanket and gazing fondly inside. I peered in again. I have never met the father, but he must be a burst melodeon.

I made the tea while baby-related conversation continued apace in the corner. Several times, the CO tried to rope me in, figuring either that there was strength in numbers, or that I am a better liar than she.

The basic problem with babies is a truth that is unspoken, but which every sentient adult male holds above all others.

And here it is:

All babies are ugly. Some are less ugly than others, but all are aesthetically challenged.

Bonnie-baby competitions, which were a staple of newspapers for many years, are contradictions in terms. There is no such thing as a bonnie baby, and no amount of lace, ribbon and soft lighting will persuade any sane person otherwise.

Not once have I surveyed a bonnie-babies page without an array of faces like saft tatties looking back.

It's just that Matthew was a particularly harrowing example, although I'm sure he'll grow into his looks, and probably have strings of girlfriends on either arm given another 20 years

So after the passing of what I felt was a proper period, I made my excuses and returned to my spade.

Besides, Matthew probably wasn't all that impressed with me, either.

Felicity has been back to see us several times, although on only one of those occasions has Matthew been with her. I'm pleased to report that, from what I saw briefly, he's certainly growing into his looks.

I had a couple of letters after this column appeared, one signed "A Former Fan" who couldn't believe that I didn't find babies attractive.

All I can plead is guilty. Sorry.

26. FIZZY, A MOST PLEASANT PHEASANT

Or why not all best friends are four-legged

"While feathery passion swirled, and delighted squawks rent the morning still, Fizzy would step his way across the plain, picking here and picking there."

IT HAS been an ornithological week in the howe. We have adopted a young one. The relationship has been simmering on and off since April last year, but it was confirmed this week when the adoptee pronounced himself happy with arrangements and moved in.

So I want to introduce you to Fizzy.

Fizzy the pheasant.

This is probably not what is on his passport, but it was chosen by the CO one morning as she studied him from the kitchen window and you don't argue with the CO: not when she has a whisk in her hand.

Fizzy has been a regular on the policies since his debut a couple of years ago. From the crippling shyness of pheasant youth, when he scuttled into the long grass at the merest hint of a human voice, he has emerged from his buckie and become progressively bolder and more inquisitive, but it was only last weekend that we found him in the house.

As game birds go, Fizzy is pretty game. I had left the front door open while I filled the car windscreen washers at the side of the house.

When I returned with the empty bucket just minutes later, Fizzy had hopped across the portals. From the way he was looking up and down and from side to side in that curious staccato way that game birds have, you'd have thought he was assessing the decor. He would have made a convincing estate-agent. All he lacked was the clipboard.

I ushered him outside, but he was reluctant to leave, for he hovered on the doorstep for a few moments before he hopped down on to the chukkies, ruffled his feathers and began strutting away in the huff.

Like all adoptees, Fizzy has a way of imposing himself. Last Boxing Day afternoon, while we were eating, Fizzy hopped on to the windowsill and stared in. It is very difficult to eat heartily when you're being stared at, even if you're being stared at only by a pheasant.

Fizzy has no sense of etiquette or decorum. I tried shooing him away with manic waves and determined scowls, but he simply blinked back.

The look said: "Who are you kidding?"

"For goodness sake get rid of him," said the CO.

Here's a tip. If you ever want to get rid of a pheasant, get as close as you can and whisper: "Regulo 5." It doesn't work, but it's curiously satisfying.

Anyway, we set him out a saucer of bread soaked in a little warm milk, and the CO put a few crumbs of Christmas cake at the side "for his pudding" (pathetic, really) and he hopped down quite happily to devour his festive repast.

But all existence has purpose. Life can't all be a heady whirl of saps and Christmas cake, even for a favoured pheasant such as Fizzy. And a pheasant's *raison d'être* is to produce plenty of little pheasants. A pheasant without a trail of pheasantettes is not doing the biz.

This is where Fizzy falls down. As a philanderer, he ranks somewhere between a trainspotter and a caravanner. All he needs is an anorak.

Fizzy appears not to have cracked even the most basic rules of Boy Pheasant Meets Girl Pheasant. Last summer, while all the other chap pheasants found paramours and trysting parlours in which to whisper their enchantments and enticements, Fizzy stepped about the policies untroubled by any thoughts of procreation.

While feathers and passion swirled and flew in almost every other hollow and corner, and delighted squawks and cries rent the morning still, Fizzy would step his way across the weedy plain, picking here, stopping to sniff the air, picking there.

If Fizzy were human, he would wear a bobble hat and collect car numbers.

One afternoon last July, when I was sitting out the back sunning myself and I heard the fall of scratchy footsteps on the concrete, I peered round and there was Fizzy. He had that looking-for-company look.

I put down my paper and studied him. He studied me. And his look said: Dejected. So I folded up my paper and put it down by the side of the lounger, swung out my legs and sat up.

"Women trouble?" I said, and he blinked and his head dropped. He had a half-hearted pick at the ground and then looked back at me. Right first time.

I knew exactly what the problem had been. A few weeks earlier, the CO and I had spotted two broods of other pheasants, one half-way along the back dyke and one in the top corner.

Each clearly had a pheasanty matriarch but, as far as we could see, there was only one pheasant stud, boldly strutting his stuff from one domicile to the other, wending his bigamous way back and forth, scraiching that peculiar half-cut scraich of triumph that pheasants have, and basically rubbing Fizzy's nose in his litany of shortcomings.

Who wouldn't be anxious about his pheasant-appeal with other chaps pinching far more than their fair share of the available talent?

"The thing is, Fizzy," I said, "have you set your mind to the chase? Have you done your utmost to ensure that your manly attractions are prominent and irresistible?"

He cocked his head and blinked. One of those empty, pheasant blinks. It was hard to imagine any lady pheasant swooning at Fizzy's feet.

"The thing is, Fizzy," I said, pulling the lounger closer, "maybe you're appearing too eager. Maybe you're just too anxious. If you'll take my advice, you'll play hard to get. Pay them no attention at at all. They'll be so aghast that they'll be curious. They'll soon come running."

Fizzy blinked again. I wasn't entirely sure that I was getting through.

"Women need to be shown who's boss," I said. "Be indifferent to them. Treat them with the utmost disdain. Plough your own furrow. Don't give them a second thought. They soon come to heel."

"It's your turn to make the tea," came the CO's parade-ground bellow from the depths of the house.

Fizzy and I cocked our heads and blinked.

I stood up. "Good luck, old man," I whispered.

"See you later."

Fizzy survived for one more summer after this. We discovered a carcase at the bottom corner of the policies one morning in 1996. We can't be sure that it was Fizzy, but we saw no further live sign of our two-footed chum, so the supposition is reasonable.

By that time, we had fallen heir to our dog, which put the kybosh on our plans for a decent burial. Every time we buried Fizzy, we'd walk past the back door a couple of hours later and discovered that the remains had returned.

Eventually, he was buried elsewhere, in a quiet spot resplendent in all the howe's majesty.

27. THE PHILOSOPHER'S TONE

Or why not to look down your nose at people in humble jobs

▬ ▬ ▬ ▬

His heart and mind soared with Byron and Emerson and Sartre, while his hands and feet were shackled to suitcases and shovels and coalpails.

IT HAS been a hammalesque week in the howe. On Friday morning, I had an appointment which involved meeting a business acquaintance in the foyer of an Aberdeen hotel. I like to arrive early for appointments to give me time to check the lie of the land, and thus it was on Friday.

I sat there while what seemed like half the business community of Aberdeen drifted back and forth in twos and threes, dressed in sober suits, carrying impeccable briefcases and stopping to shake hands and laugh polite laughs.

Cruising inconspicuously through all this furious briefcasing, I noticed, was a little chap in a grey-nylon overall. I'd have put him in his late 50s. No one paid him any attention, as far as I could see. Neither did he acknowledge anyone else. For all the conversing going on around him and over his head, he said nary a word.

He would appear at one end of the foyer carrying a screwdriver, weave his way silently through knots of people, and disappear at the other end. Then he would reappear, carrying maybe a box of paper towels or a handful of light bulbs, retrace his former route and disappear once more. Back he would come, this time carrying perhaps a suitcase. A few moments later, with maybe a tray of sandwiches, there he was again.

No one reacted. Neither did he react. He might have been invisible to all but me, for all I knew; a leprechaun in a grey-nylon overall. He was the establishment's example of that little-sung breed, the hotel porter.

Hotel porters have a pretty rough time of it. It's not all holding our your hand for tips and lounging behind the scenes reading the paper. Porters are only one step above dogsbodies in tourism's evolutionary chain. I know. I had a job for two teenage summers as a porter at a Highland hotel. It was there that I met Charlie. We'll call him Charlie, although that was not his real name.

Charlie was a philosophical Glaswegian in his mid-50s, of Jewish extraction, who had built his life on a succession of short-term jobs travelling round Scotland. A few days' cutting wood here, a week's fencing there. Grouse-beating. Picking fruit. Lifting tatties. Clearing snow. Charlie's year was governed by the seasons. Anyone who has worked in a hotel will know someone like him.

He was one of those people blessed with a brilliant mind and quick wit who had never found a career fitting his talents, but who was unperturbed by it because he had found far better riches. Charlie had found serenity and contentment.

I never heard Charlie swear. Nor did I hear him complain. I never heard him criticise another soul, even although he, more than most, had good reason. He did whatever was required of him, and a wee bit more besides, with stoicism and good humour.

He was also one of the best-read men I have met. He could quote the classics and be letter-perfect. He had a bon mot for every occasion. His heart and mind soared with Byron and Emerson and Sartre, while his hands and feet were shackled to suitcases and shovels and coalpails.

In my second summer at the hotel, Charlie turned up at the stillroom door as usual in the third week of June. The housemaids used to say you could set your watch by Charlie's arrival. Hotel managers, apparently, had marked off that fourth Saturday in June every year on the calendar, even although no formal arrangement had been made because, after all, Charlie was dependable.

This particular year, a new manager, unaware of the unspoken contract between Charlie and the hotel, had already employed what he felt was a sufficient number of seasonal porters. And, no, he wasn't able to justify another, no matter what tradition might demand. Tradition didn't square the books.

The only position he could offer was as a kitchen porter, washing the pots, on a split shift. There would be one day off a week and the money would have to be considerably less, reflecting the smaller responsibility and the fact that he would not be presenting a public image.

Charlie accepted, although we could see that he was disappointed. It was not that he felt that washing pots was beneath him, but his routine had been disturbed, and creatures of habit, as Charlie was, don't care for that.

So he stood over the sink, night after humid night, condensation running down his bald head; the sweat stains under his oxters spread across his back and chest as each evening wore on.

At the end of dinner service, when the last light in the kitchen had been switched off and waitresses had gone home or were putting up their feet and having a fag, Charlie would still be at station over the stillroom sink, wielding steel wool and industrial bottles of Doby. Those were the times, when an evening's end was drawing near, that he could be coaxed to chat about the old days.

"There's plenty tricks tae the poarter's trade, son," he would say. He sounded a lot like Bill Shankly, now that I think of it. And he would begin itemising the little mischiefs which earned him a wee bit extra in tips. When handing back receipt and change on a platter, he said, always make your thumb catch on the receipt. Customers pick up a receipt before they pick up cash. If the receipt "sticks", they are more likely to let a few coins "stick", too, in their fluster. And I could imagine Charlie nodding and smiling silent and sincere thanks to such tippers.

I tried it once or twice. It never worked.

When someone phones down asking for room service after the kitchen has shut for the night, never say: "All right", or: "Right away." Always say: "Well, I'll see what I can do", with a note of dubiety.

Then sit back for 15 minutes and read the paper.   Make up the sandwiches or whatever and take them up to the room. The customer thinks you've been to an immense amount of trouble and this is reflected in the tip.

Charlie was full of such hints that summer. Denied the chance to practise them himself, he shared them with an amateur, keen to see that tradition was observed.

Mostly, Charlie's hints didn't work for me; more a reflection on the practitioner than the practice. But I never let on; I didn't have the heart. Charlie, after all, was bringing on the next generation; passing down time-honoured skills.

I haven't seen him in almost 20 years. He'll be in his mid-70s now. He could be doing his rounds still, although maybe a little less able to humph vast portmanteaux along corridors; a little less inclined to assemble cots at short notice, or clean grates, or hang curtains, or stack firewood.

He might have retired to a hostel for the homeless. He might have settled down to while away his days with books. We can't overlook the possibility that he might have passed over.

But if you meet him, see if you can engage him in conversation. You won't regret it. And if you do meet him, perhaps you could let me know.

<hr />

I never did locate Charlie again. I had two, perhaps three, letters and one phone call from people who felt they had met someone fitting the description, but none of the tipoffs checked out.

One of the housemaids who had worked at the hotel at the same time got in touch to say that she thought Charlie had died in the cold winter of 79, although we couldn't pin that down, either.

Still looking.

28. STATING THE OBVIOUS

Or how to spot a son or daughter of the North-east

▬▬ ▬▬ ▬▬ ▬▬

"Stating the obvious acknowledges the existence of the
other person in a friendly, open way that will not offend,
be controversial or start a shouting match."

IT HAS been a cynosural week in the howe. One of the great
things about staying in the country among your ain fowk and
talking your ain tongue is the comforting familiarity of rural
ritual.

I'm thinking not of grand rural ritual, such as the agricultural
show, the hairst, the Saturday-morning sale of work in the village
hall, the summer evening treasure hunt, lambing time, blocked
roads and the ferlies gathering for a news round the phone box.

I'm thinking more of a rural ritual which is so omnipresent that
none of us gives it a second thought. It comes so naturally to
anyone born and brought up in the rural North-east, irrespective
of vintage, that it doesn't really occur to us.

I see it in my parents and their friends, and saw it in my
grandparents and their contemporaries. I find it in myself in
unguarded moments and I hope, will be able to see it ultimately
in those who are but saplings yet.

It's our fondness for stating the obvious.

The whole principle occurred to me last Sunday afternoon when
I had tried to judge the gaps in the thunderstorms to allow me to
do the standard three-mile walk with the dog and stay moderately
dry.

On a brisk tour, the circuit takes 55 minutes. It takes slightly longer if we meet cars, for he has been trained to sit down when he hears an engine, which works a treat and amuses motorists into the bargain. However, if other dogs have done the circuit within the previous three hours, the 55 minutes can lengthen by half as much again, for any self-respecting dog must sniff and explore trails which others have blazed.

With so many variables, accurate timing of a walk is nigh impossible and, unfortunately, on the afternoon in question, all the calculations went awry. The weather closed in when we were barely two-thirds of the way round. "Thunderstorm" hardly seems to convey the blinding viciousness of what was falling about us.

We were passing through a small hamlet, water stotting from the tarmac and drains gurgling merrily, when we spied a woman in her 50s approaching on the other side of the road.

"Aye, aye," she said. "Rain again."

I agreed with her and we went our separate ways. It was a good minute later, with the precipitation bouncing six inches off the road, the Esset Burn in full spate, the dog's legs buckling because of the weight of water in his coat, and blacker than black clouds emptying faster and faster that the smile crept across my face.

"Aye," I said to myself. "Rain again."

Stating the obvious in the Doric takes many forms, but the purpose is always the same. If you imagine these exchanges are meant to convey useful information, you're mistaken. The real purpose is social intercourse. Stating the obvious acknowledges the existence of the other person in a friendly, open way that will not offend, be controversial or start a shouting match.

Hence, the CO and I will be wandering around a superstore in Aberdeen comparing prices and examining ingredients labels; I manoeuvring a laden trolley with food enough for a convention of fatties, when another couple from the howe will appear in the same aisle.

"Aye, aye," they'll say. "Ye're deein the messages."

Or, as I've written before, we'll be out for a romantic stroll in the autumn gloaming when, away at the other end of a long, straight stretch, we'll see the form of someone walking towards us.

As the distance between us narrows over the next 10 minutes, and we establish who it is and what we might say as conversation, you can be sure that as soon as he is within speaking distance he will observe: "Aye, ye're oot for a walk."

Before I get too cocky, I should confess that last night, as I was walking through the Press and Journal office at around 5.30, I bumped into a colleague who had hauled on his coat, was carrying a paper and was heading towards the car-park door.

"Well, Jim," I said, "that's you finished again."

In the 1960s, when we had finished our 6pm repast, my mother would begin gathering the dishes from the table and announce: "Well, we've had our tea."

Frequently, my father would return home after a fortnight and be told: "It was Wullie's funeral last Thursday."

Always he would reply: "Is Wullie deid?"

In my reporting days in the late 1970s we had an editorial pool fleet of notoriously unreliable HC Vauxhall Vivas. I was out with a photographer on Deeside one summer afternoon when there was crunch, a bang and a sound of extreme mechanical sickness from under the bonnet,

Bob, the photographer, stopped, flipped the bonnet and we both peered in. I suggested that we call the company garage, but Bob was certain that the problem was minor and that he could fix it in minutes.

Fifteen minutes later, with oily marks up to his elbows and language of an increasingly fluorescent nature filling the engine cavity, an old Hillman Hunter drew alongside and an elderly chap in a bunnet, with the ruddy complexion of a retired man of the soil, leaned across the passenger seat and wound down the window.

Bob, clarted in grease and swearing profusely, looked up from the depths of the engine. I, much cleaner but just as frustrated, looked up, too. Almost before the man opened his mouth, I knew what was coming.

"Hiv ye broken doon?"

Only once have I heard an adverse reaction to stating the obvious, and that was in Aberdeen. Sorry, Aberdeen.

It was four or five years ago at a busy filling station on one of the main arterial routes into the city.

On the day in question, the station had just installed new computer equipment or had a very green operator on duty but, in any case a queue of six or seven people had built up while the assistant struggled to cope with technology that was refusing to co-operate.

Most of us were perfectly calm about it, for the young woman was clearly flustered, embarrassed and apologetic, although her supervisor's lack of interest needled one or two of the people in front of me, particularly a wiry wee lady in her 60s who looked as if she might not stand for any nonsense from anyone.

After fully five minutes, we could see a portly gentleman in three-piece suit approaching from the pumps where he had just filled his Mercedes.

He opened the door into the filling-station shop and stopped dead in his tracks, bewildered by the snake of seven people in front of him. "Is this a queue?" he said.

The wiry wee woman shot him a glare. "No," she snapped. "It's an elephant."

The mail after this column was most entertaining. Among other true tales, a former assistant from a Banff chip shop reported an elderly customer arriving at the head of the queue at the height of a busy Friday evening and asking: "Ony chips?"

There was also a sheepish admission from a Fyvie woman. She recounted being ushered through to a front room at Turriff to see her late uncle laid oot and hearing herself saying: "Isn't that jist him?"

29. NOT SO MEAN CUISINE

Or why to give airline caterers a little credit

*"Airlines are on a culinary hiding to nothing. It amazes
me that they manage the minor miracles they do. Airline
food isn't as bad as pseuds would have you believe."*

IT HAS been an esculent week in the howe. We have been
marvelling at the current media obsession with food. There is
scarcely an hour in the television day when a cookery
programme of some sort is not being broadcast. There is scarcely
a newspaper or magazine that does not have a recipe in every
issue.

Now network radio has announced that it intends to increase its
culinary output.

Who is watching, reading and listening to all this cookery?
People who can't abide the demands of the kitchen won't be
interested, and those who quiver with excitement at being wrist-
deep in dough will want to be filling their hours doing exactly
that.

Or does it just reflect the fact that we have become more
interested in the politics of our food and in our health; both factors
which have spilled over into what otherwise would be just a
collection of recipes?

The public's palate has become more finicky of late. With many
years of foreign holidays under many belts, most of the population
is more inclined to explore the full culinary cornucopia.

The days when a luxury pudding was a spoonful of jam in your tapioca, and roughage was the crust on school macaroni, are sadly behind us. Now, unless a dish contains jalapena, pesto or piri-piri, much of the younger set will turn up their so-sophisticated noses. Skirlie is anathema to these poor lost souls.

Don't even mention stovies.

Such raised expectations pose new and ever-greater dilemmas for those who would serve the public their food and try to satisfy their new, boundless culinary horizons. The dilemma is nowhere more pronounced than with airlines.

Consider the problem. An airline has to devise menus for food which will stand storage, transportation and microwaved reheating.

Like every other restaurateur, the airline must keep to a strict budget. The completed meals must be eaten in confined spaces with comparatively few of the normal cookery implements.

They must not be so malodorous that other passengers will be put off. They must look attractive in the most unattractive tinfoil trays.

In short, airlines are on a culinary hiding to nothing, and it amazes me consistently that they manage the minor miracles they do. Whisper it, but I don't think that airline food is as bad as the braying pseuds would have you believe.

Airline food is simply an easy target for the hard-of-thinking, and generally an unjustified one, given the circumstances in which the meals must be produced and the criteria they must fit. Any passenger expecting Le Manoir aux Quat' Saisons at 37,000ft deserves to be disappointed.

Which is not to say that I haven't had bad airline meals, because I have. I have tackled a portion of spinach that looked suspiciously like baked dung; an omelette that would have made a very fetching purse, and a piece of cheddar that would have kept a three-year-old entertained for a morning.

But, then, I have had even worse meals while sitting at ground level, when the chef could not have made the excuse that his kitchen was travelling at 520mph.

As if to prove how impossible it is for airlines to meet the demands of passengers, I have in front of me the results of a tasting session which was conducted by Continental Airlines. This Houston-based carrier invited some of its frequent fliers to preview its new-season dishes and to seek their opinions.

The comments come in many forms and pitched at many levels of expertise, but the one I'm sure Continental's chefs appreciated was from a Dorothy Moore, 29, who complains that the smoked salmon is "too fishy".

I have seen sullenness of both sides of the customer-restaurant divide. I have squirmed with embarrassment when an interviewee studied very theatrically the menu in a vegetarian restaurant and demanded imperiously to know if the establishment served food.

I have watched, bemused, when a restaurant served up blatant oven chips when its menu promised the real thing, and listened to the impatient sighs and mutterings of the waitress when this was pointed out.

I have seen what restaurants do behind the scenes to the food of difficult customers, and I don't care what assurances the environmental-health regulations are supposed to offer, because I have seen it happen — in glorious Technicolor. I'll spare you the details, in case you are eating while you read.

And I know none of you will believe this, but the CO will back me up; we were once sitting at breakfast in a London hotel when an American doctor clapped his hands at the next table and the maître D scuttled over.

"Yes, Dr Globus?"

"Could you tell me why the waiter has placed the toast rack to my left, instead of to my right, which you know I prefer?"

The poor waiter was hauled across and berated vehemently, to Dr Globus's satisfaction.

Who would be a restaurateur?

Come to think of it, who would be a customer?

Which brings me to the final stories. I know perfectly well that they are works of complete fiction, but they were told to me many years ago by a retired chef and they amused me then and they amuse me still.

A Scot went into a London restaurant, studied the surroundings and then walked slowly to a table and sat down.

Presently, a waiter came across. "Tell me," said the Scot, "fit can I eat for ma money the day?"

The waiter handed over the menu and said: "Here you are. You can order anything in there."

The Scot ordered a three-course meal, with coffee and a dram and was presented with a bill for £7 12s 6d (this was a long time ago, you understand).

So the Scot took a pound from his pocket, handed it to the waiter and got up to go. "There you are," he said, "I asked ye fit I could eat for ma money, and this is aa the money I've got."

The second tale concerns a poor Scottish Catholic family with eight children who wandered into a plush Glasgow restaurant in the 1930s.

"Is it richt that the breid's free in this restaurant?" said the man.

"Yes," said the waiter.

"Then bring us ten servings of your finest breid." The waiter was horrified and complained to the manager about such brass neck.

"Leave him to me," said the boss, who went across to the table.

"Are you the boss?" said the Scot.

"I am."

"OK, what's happened to the string quartet today?"

If ever you're in the company of waiters or waitresses, get them to tell you about the things diners try to secrete in their handbags.

You'd expect leftover bits of steak to be wrapped up in napkins and taken away, but I know of one hotel where a customer was spotted trying to snaffle the table decoration, complete with candles and miniature fountain.

30. MILK OF AMNESIA

Or how to . . . um . . . wait a minute; it'll come back to me

████ ████ ████ ████

"Absent-mindedness was 'simply a brain trying to cope
with too much and, thus, shutting down certain areas
temporarily for the sake of self-preservation'."

IT HAS been a Lethean week in the howe. I was in the queue at the bank on Monday morning, looking idly at my feet and wondering if I should tell the woman in front that she had an unsightly aperture in her tights, when it happened again.

It occurred to me in a hot flash that I had no idea what I was doing there. It was a bank, certainly, so presumably I had intended to conduct some financial transaction or other, but I was bereft of cheques, cashcard or any other banky paraphernalia.

Perspiring and rummaging in all my pockets for clues, it was fully 20 seconds before I remembered that I was there to deposit cheques, and another 10 seconds before I realised that I had left them, two miles away, still at home on a kitchen worktop.

I let slip the little involuntary groan that is customary on these occasions and departed the bank. I could hear a small commotion and confusion behind me as I left, but I knew the bank staff would be explaining to other customers that there was no cause for alarm: it was just the absent-minded man again.

I call it absent-mindedness. The CO calls it incipient senility.

I can dispute with the utmost vigour any suggestion of senility, however, now that I have read the research findings of an eminent US psychologist, who was featured a couple of months ago in an

American weekly news magazine. I would name him, but I forget where I put the magazine.

He asserted that, except for physiological problems, absent-mindedness was "simply a manifestation of a brain that is trying to cope with too much and, thus, shuts down certain areas temporarily for the sake of self-preservation".

He went on to report that likely sufferers can be spotted in childhood because of three factors.

The first of the three factors was a propensity for day-dreaming. The child who gazes out of the classroom window will become the adult who needs his mittens tied at either end of a long string and threaded up his sleeves.

The second of the three factors was a compulsion to keep records and to write things down, so that nothing may go astray, leaving the child feeling vulnerable and exposed. He could have been describing my whole primary-school career.

And the third factor . . . actually, I forget what the third factor was, but it was a good one.

The CO delights in regaling fellow-guests at functions with my latest amnesiac episodes. She does it, she says, because it breaks the ice. She could wear a funny hat, but she prefers to make her husband an object of derision and scorn.

Few among our acquaintances can't have heard of the time I loaded the boot of the car with two black bags of rubbish, intending to decant them into the wheelie-bin at the end of the drive and them proceed into work. Alas, by the time I got to the end of the drive I had forgotten all about them. The car grew increasingly stinky for more than a week before I traced the problem to source.

A couple of weeks ago, the washer bottles on the car ran dry on the way home, so I parked outside the kitchen window, propped up the bonnet and went to get the bottle of washer fluid and a bucket of water.

I found the bottle of fluid under the back sink and noticed, while I was there, that a bag of washing powder had spilled, so I began tidying up that. I brushed together the last of the remains and took the dustpan to the bucket at the back door.

While there, I noticed that the loganberries were looking a little dry around the roots, so I went into the garage for a roozer. I watered the loganberries, then I returned to the kitchen to have my tea. I was half-way through the meal when I looked out and wondered how my car had come to have its bonnet up.

There are risks to admitting failings professionally, but the passage of time makes this safer than most. I hope.

Twenty years ago, when I was a reporter, I was assigned to interview a mountain-rescue team leader who lived in Aberdeen.

I did everything a keen young reporter should do. I did the research in our library, gathered my thoughts and planned out the likely lines of discussion. I established what length the story might make and advised the newsdesk accordingly. I asked the picture editor to arrange photographs. Finally, I signed out a pool car and drove off into the city. I was half-way downtown before it hit me:

I hadn't a clue where I was going.

I pulled into the side of the street and sat for five minutes trying desperately to recall where I was meant to be. Ultimately, I had to swallow my pride and phone HQ. "Hello, it's Norman here. Where was I going?"

"Belvidere Crescent," said a colleague, and — this is the really irksome bit — he said it in that monotone which betrayed that he was not in the least surprised.

Last month, the CO and I had to rush home from a Saturday in Aberdeen, dicht our nibs, dust our oxters and change, then rush back to the city again to attend the retirement party of a colleague who had done sterling service for the paper for 33 years.

We were rather ambitious in our timings in any case, but as we passed the city boundary, I looked at my watch and said: "I think we're going to arrive in the middle of the speeches. I hate arriving in the middle of something. It's very disrespectful."

We bowled into the hotel car park and, half-running and half-stytering, raced up the steps and through the front door of one of Aberdeen's better establishments.

With several function suites to its name, it should have had a direction board or some such, but it didn't, so I collared a young man in uniform and said: "Watson function?"

He looked puzzled and shook his head.

"The Press and Journal?" I said.

"Mandy?" he shouted across the foyer. "Watson function? Press and Journal?"

Mandy looked equally puzzled.

And just as she was looking puzzled, I realised that I had arrived at the wrong hotel.

The CO agrees that I promised her life would never be boring, but says she would settle for just five minutes of plain sailing every so often, just to remind her how normal wives live.

I have explained that there is very little that I can do about it. Absent-mindedness and I have been bedfellows for more than 40 years and we have come to an understanding.

Those of you who suffer know what I mean. Meanwhile, last night, I smelled paint coming from the garage. There, I found the CO making up a placard and threading string through the two holes. It reads:

If found wandering, please return to:
Mrs Harper
The Howe

⬛ ⬛ ⬛ ⬛

This is the great thing about Press and Journal readers. On other newspapers, columnists confessing to forgetfulness get letters and phone calls telling them how stupid they are.

I got three dozen sheepish admissions from people — some of them eminent in their professions — who were just as prone to absent-mindedness and whose colleagues were convinced that they were raving mad. Honestly, it cheers you up.

31. TROUBLE AT THE TEAROOM

Or why you should avoid the least friendly cafe in Scotland

▬ ▬ ▬ ▬

*"The food was excellent and the surroundings impeccably
clean, but you wonder why someone with such a dislike of
humanity sets up a business to serve humans."*

I T HAS been an uncomplaisant week in the howe. You'll have
noticed all the fuss about Scottish tourism. Quite rightly, it is
lauded as the country's biggest earner, bringing millions upon
millions of pounds into the national coffers and knocking into a
cocket hat everything from light engineering to printed circuits to
call centres.

You'll have noticed, also, that there have been fewer foreign-
registered cars on Scottish roads this year; something which has
been attributed to a nasty combination of inflated sterling, bad
weather and the collapse of whichever has been the latest world
economy to go belly-up.

Which means, in turn, that you'll have been paying attention to
the various strategies which the Scottish industry is developing to
try to salvage something from a dreadful summer season. That
encompasses everything from discount deals, extra hotel nights at
no extra cost, money-off vouchers and a campaign to persuade
Scots to try a stay-at-home break.

Judging by the empty clang, too many Scots have taken the
advice literally and have stayed resolutely by their own firesides.

Critics have accused parts of the industry of being deeply
unfriendly towards their customers; of regarding clients as a

necessary nuisance; of not realising that negativity breeds antipathy and leads, in turn, to dwindling income.

I'm stressing *parts* of the industry but, as in every trade, it's such parts that spoil the whole, and we all know that stories of bad encounters bear retelling time and time again, while pleasant encounters usually dissolve within a couple of weeks into a private, satisfied glow.

Some of you will be aware that the Press and Journal has been carrying an exchange of readers' letters in which some correspondents have accused Highlanders of being unfriendly, and Highlanders have rushed to defend themselves and their compatriots with equal conviction.

"The only people who think Highlanders are friendly are Highlanders themselves," is one reader's quotation which sticks in my memory.

"Not all tourist establishments in the Highlands are run by Highlanders," was an equally frustrated response.

I am not getting involved in generalisations and inter-necine warfare, but it brought to mind what was probably the unfriendliest tearoom in Scotland and, yes, it was in the Highlands, although it could equally have been anywhere else, I'm sure.

With three pensioners in our charge, we had ventured on a Saturday jaunt to Inverness and points north and west. At the approach of fly-cup time, signalled with Greenwich-pips accuracy by the creaks and rumbles from three elderly stomachs in the back seat ("Are you hungry?" "Not really." *Rrrrooooooarrrrr*. "Well, maybe we could manage a wee something") we headed for the centre of a small town.

It was too early for lunch and too late for breakfast, so we looked for a tearoom that was reasonably clean and popular, but not so popular that it was packed and uncomfortable.

Since you should always let pensioners choose tearooms, because they have a nose for that sort of thing, the CO and I found ourselves trailed off the main street and up a busy side road. Outside what looked like a converted steading stood an A-board on the pavement, promising untold culinary delights within.

I noticed before we entered that as well as the usual credit-card logos crowded in the glass of the door, a standard 3x5 lined index card had been tacked on near the handle. It bore the legend:

Wipe Your Feet

All five of us did a soft-shoe shuffle on the coconut mat and trooped inside. We found ourselves in a lobby and saw, through an interior glassed door, about a dozen tables dressed in blue gingham and about half a dozen patrons seated in ones and twos and horsing into scones. All were elderly — an excellent sign.

We were about to step into the dining-room when I noticed another 3x5 card tacked on the door. It read:

Wait To Be Seated

So we waited. And we waited. And we waited. By the time it was clear that there was a greater chance of sighting a Yeti than sighting a waitress, we had become the objects of great interest among those who had actually managed to be seated already.

Unable to bear it any longer, I grasped the door handle and stepped inside, whereupon an ample matron descended as if from nowhere and said: "Yes?"

It was difficult to know how to answer her. Evidently, it hadn't occurred to her why strangers would visit a tearoom.

"We were waiting to be seated," I said.

"Five?"

"Yes."

She turned inside and stood by a table for five. While we were settling, I noticed something I had not seen anywhere before and have not seen anywhere since. The whole room was littered with 3x5 cards bearing instructions and commands. Wall pictures had cards slotted into their frames advising:

Do Not Touch

Beside the curtains was tacked a card reading:

Do Not Open Window

On an old sideboard, a card commanded:

Do Not Self-Select Cutlery

A door at the far corner carried a card which announced:

Private. No Entry. Staff Only.

On the wall beside us was a card which declared:

Toilet Facilities For Patrons Only. Ask Waitress For Key

Inside the front cover of the menu was slipped a 3x5 card advising:

Last Breakfast Orders Strictly 9.15am

There were dozens more, advising everything from the fact that adults could not order child portions, to the fact that breakages "may be chargeable". We had stumbled into the Stalag Luft Kozy Koffee Korner.

The food was excellent and the surroundings impeccably clean. Even the service, when it came, was efficient, if a little brusque. But you wonder why someone with such an intense dislike of humanity bothers setting up a business to serve humans.

The point is that all five of us have long since forgotten the good points and what we remember, above all, is "that tearoom with all the instructions".

I wish I could report the existence of a 3x5 card that completed the comic effect, but it would not be true. She should really have had one tacked to the inside of the front door so that departing guests could read:

Have A Nice Day

━━ ━━ ━━ ━━

The owners of the tearoom did not respond, but I got dozens of hot tips from readers about various places to try next time we were in the Inverness area. We're working our way through them slowly.

32. GAEL WARNING

Or why Doric-speakers should learn a lesson from our Celtic cousins

▬ ▬ ▬ ▬

*"Doric-speakers should have been learning the tactics
which won Gaels such spectacular results and applying
them with equal vigour."*

IT HAS been a diglot week in the howe. Like most of you, I have spent the past several days attending various family functions, various private functions and one or two public functions, albeit in a private capacity.

It happened that one of these functions was held but a few miles from Gaeldom, where the topic exercising minds and tempers was Highland Council's apparent first step to diminish its commitment to Gaelic and thereby save a few thousand pounds.

Highland Council has been convening public focus groups to gauge which of its services could most stand a budget cut and generate least protest. Gaelic has not been scoring well.

While Highland Council couched the terms and purpose of its focus-group activities somewhat tentatively, the reaction among Gaels has been more than fiery. You don't fight for finance and for cultural recognition for as long as Gaels did, and then shrug shoulders when a threat appears.

Days later, I attended a function just a few miles away from the howe. Gaelic-speakers were scarce, as you would understand, yet the principal topic of conversation again was the apparently burgeoning threat to Gaelic-medium education in the Highlands.

Some were sympathetic, but I would be lying if I put the

number at more than half a dozen. By far the majority reaction was that Gaeldom had enjoyed lavish public patronage for too long at the expense of other cultures, and that it should bear its share of the realities of public finance.

Which is where I differ from my Doric brothers and sisters.

I differ not in the matter of public finance in the Highlands, which is the business of Highland Council and the taxpayers of the Highlands; not for exploring here.

Instead, I'm puzzled by the curious enmity that has festered between Gaelic and the Doric for too long. Much of this traffic has been one way. Far from taking vicarious delight in another culture's gathering storm, Doric-speakers should be concerned about the health of all other minority cultures.

Far from resenting the funds which Gaeldom has wrought from the public purse, and its compulsory quota of Gaelic programming on radio and television, Doric-speakers should have been learning the tactics which won Gaels such spectacular results and applying them with equal vigour.

Whining at another's success is a mark of pettiness, equalled only by unconcealed glee when the success seems to be jeopardised. You promote your culture by promoting your culture, which is what Gaels did vigorously and persistently. You don't promote it by carping across fences and sulking in tents.

Gaelic faces a greater struggle than some Gaels appear to think. The first public expression of resentment has fallen as music on ears much farther afield than the Highlands. In some ways, this might be taken as a tribute to the efficacy of Gaelic campaigning in the past. Only the most successful earn the most resentment.

At a recent festive function, I happened to meet a BBC-type person from the Central Belt. She would not claim to be a household name, but she is certainly a medium-to-big wheel in Scottish broadcasting, whose credit appears on many home-produced programmes.

She believes that many of the ills of Scottish broadcasting could be cured if its throat were freed of what she described as the strangling clutch of "Gaels and their quota".

Her view, expressed with no small vehemence, was that a

schedule peppered with Gaelic programming to serve the interests of less than 1% of the population diminished the service to the remaining 99%.

I'm sure it's a common view in Scottish broadcasting, but I'm not sure that you can justify or refuse to justify a culture on simple arithmetic. It is hard to defend heritage on fourpence ha'penny.

It's only marginally easier on £20million, or whatever the latest Gaelic broadcasting subsidy is.

Which brings me to my most bizarre encounter with Gaelic. It indicates that nothing in the public presentation of a culture and its adherents is entirely what it seems.

In the 1980s, I sat on an awards jury for the Television and Radio Industries Club of Scotland. The awards that year were sponsored by the BBC and I was invited, with several English media notables and one other Scot, to sit on the judging panel for radio programming. I thought the national mix on the jury was curious, but that's another story.

I was charged with spending three weeks listening to several dozen tapes of radio programmes which had been produced in Scotland in the previous 12 months. Radio is one of the greatest media pleasures, but the delight palls when listening is compulsory and against deadline.

I listened in the shower, in the car, over lunch and before I fell asleep. I listened to the documentaries about the Darien Gap, pheasant-breeding and the River Tweed. I listened to morning-music shows filled with music no one in their right ear would call music. I heard talks about Napier and Robert Watson Watt.

I listened to dramas which confirmed only how traumatised the writers must have been in childhood (doesn't anyone write stories any more? Must they all be psychological studies or rants about social deprivation?)

And one of the entries was a programme entirely in Gaelic.

The jury convened at Broadcasting House, Glasgow, one Thursday morning, and we began working through eight or nine different award categories, each with four or five nominations.

After lunch, we came to the category in which the Gaelic programme appeared. One of the English jurors declared immediately that she could not judge the programme as she did not speak Gaelic. I asked to be excused the entire category because by being unable to judge one, I could not fairly judge all.

I won't trouble you with the deliberations which ensued, but the Gaelic programme won.

With mounting disbelief, I realised from the discussions among the remaining jurors, that not one of them could speak Gaelic. I couldn't decide whether to be annoyed at the event committee for not having had foresight to appoint a Gaelic-speaking juror, or with my fellow-judges for pressing on with a farcical adjudication.

What lives with me most clearly is the manner in which the presiding judge, a highly respected English critic, fought to justify a nonsensical decision. When my fellow-protester wondered how judges who did not have Gaelic could sit in judgment on a programme presented entirely in Gaelic, the president said: "But creating an atmosphere is the essence of radio. They sound so enthusiastic. Don't you think they are enjoying themselves? Don't you think that enthusiasm will have communicated to listeners?"

Quite apart from being stupefyingly patronising, by that philosophy we might as well have been giving an award to a tape of elephants mating.

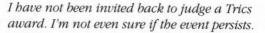

I have not been invited back to judge a Trics award. I'm not even sure if the event persists.

Saddest of all, there's a production team somewhere in the Highlands and Islands proudly displaying a trophy for the quality of their work, presumably unaware that the people who judged that work couldn't understand a word in their entire programme.

33. GRAVE CONCERNS

Or why there are hundreds of tales in every cemetery

▬ ▬ ▬ ▬

*"Barring a public library, there are more human stories in
a row of gravestone inscriptions than anywhere else. It
stimulates the imagination to an incredible degree."*

IT HAS been an exequious week in the howe. For several
months, I had managed to go cold turkey. With
encouragement from Mrs Harper and a steady nerve, I had
suffered remarkably few withdrawal symptoms, but on Saturday
evening I undid all the rehabilitation work of the last couple of
months and yielded to temptation.

I visited a graveyard.

Consider it one of my curious compulsions, but if I spot a
cemetery, I have to go in. Wherever we go on holiday, I track
down the burial ground and pay my respects. Some tourists claim
that the quickest way to learn the truth about any city is to visit its
cafés, theatres and restaurants. I say visit a supermarket, travel on
a bus and find a graveyard and you know all you need to know.

During our disastrous holiday in Portugal in April, while other
people were streaked out on the beach, flat out in bars or doing
the rounds of the street markets, I was communing with the souls
of the departed in the Portimão necropolis.

"It's like living with the Addams Family," Mrs Harper whispers to
her friends when I am out of the room.

My favourite is the Glasgow Necropolis, which is so ridiculously
Gothic and imposing that it might have been created by a set-

designer for a horror film. All it needs is a carpet of dry-ice smoke, a flash of blue lighting every so often and a rumble of thunder and it's half-way to an Oscar nomination.

Joint second are the Jewish Cemetery in Newington, Edinburgh; Tomnahurich in Inverness, and the Trinity Cemetery, Aberdeen. There is nothing particularly imposing in their settings, but I find their atmospheres affecting,

For small rural cemeteries with incredibly heavy atmosphere, visit Ythanwells, Corgarff or almost any on the edges of Mearns villages.

For a cemetery to unnerve you, try walking through the southern half of Allenvale, Aberdeen, in the last half-hour before darkness, particularly in the central area where the trees are now so mature that they meet overhead and almost obscure everything beneath.

To strike you silent and make you feel incredibly humble, the larger war cemeteries in Normandy are utterly moving. All parents should take their teenagers to see one at least once and to explain.

Like many a suffering wife who cannot fathom her husband's little mortal weaknesses but tolerates them all the same, Mrs Harper sits resolutely in the car outside the cemetery gates on occasions such as these. She says that graveyards give her the creeps and that, as we'll all be planted in one soon enough, she has no wish to spend what few waking years she has hovering about headstones.

But she misunderstands the appeal of graveyards. I go not for a shiver up the back or, these days, to trip over drug-addicts. I wouldn't even claim that I go for the peace and the solitude, although I find that a visit to my grandparents every so often is remarkably calming.

I go because, barring a public library, there are more human stories in a row of gravestone inscriptions than anywhere else. It stimulates the imagination to an incredible degree. I challenge anyone to walk more than a dozen paces down any avenue in any cemetery and not to wonder at the lives represented on at least one tombstone.

On Saturday evening, we went back to Allenvale in Aberdeen

because I had never seen the memorial to James Scott Skinner, son of Deeside and king of the strathspey and reel. It was every bit as imposing as I had been told, and I'm glad that I went.

But the other stories were intriguing, too. There was a widow who had died, aged 94, at the turn of the century. She had been predeceased by her 28-year-old husband 70 years before. That's a long time a widow. How lonely a life did she have, I wonder? How did she make ends meet?

There was a 22-year-old trawlerman who was drowned in the 1890s, leaving behind his 48-year-old wife. What could have been the story of that courtship?

There was the man of 38 who appeared to have died five days after the death of his twins in the 1920s. Grief? Disease? Or something darker?

None of these stories has a ready answer now, which makes them all the more compelling and intriguing. At Ythanwells, there is a stone against the back wall telling of an entire family of adults, teenagers and children being wiped out over the space of a few days, which was presumably the tragic effect of contagion.

At Alford, there is a stone commemorating an aged couple who passed away with only two or three days between them and which carries the inscription:

In Death They Were Not Divided

My favourite is at Allenvale. It reads:

Life with him was an adventure

What a man he must have been to have inspired that in his family. Would that we could all be remembered the same way.

I have often wondered what I would like on my own tombstone when the time comes. For a while, I quite fancied: "I knew something like this would happen" or: "And what do you think you're looking at?", but I've grown past that belligerent stage.

Mrs Harper says hers should read: "She had a lot to put up with."

I have vetoed that, mainly because no wife of a writer, especially a wife who is a graduate in English, can have an epitaph which ends in a preposition.

So her gravestone will not have that on.

Discussions will likely continue for some years yet, Deo volente. Meanwhile, we trust that our ceremonial parting, when it comes, will be a little more ordered than the burial of one of my uncles at Tomnahurich, Inverness, several Decembers ago.

The Doric contingent had travelled up to the Highland capital under separate cover. We attended the service and went to the graveside then, once formalities had been concluded, held back while the Highland contingent paid their respects.

With a few stragglers remaining, my mother and aunt stepped forward to read the wreath tributes, as mothers and aunts do.

Unfortunately, my mother hadn't noticed that only a piece of green baize, not unlike the artificial grass you see on a greengrocer's apple display, had been stretched across the lair for temporary cover, with some of the wreaths on top. The grave had not been filled in.

She stepped forward to read the card on one inaccessible wreath and, with a rumble and thump, disappeared from view.

As we rushed to haul her out, hoping that no one had noticed, she struggled to beach herself above ground once again.

"Well," she said with that curious haughty sniff of mothers who pretend that a catastrophe just past has never actually happened and that their dignity remains intact, "that's the closest I've been to him in twenty-five years."

━━ ━━ ━━ ━━

Two neighbours told me recently of a gravestone at the cemetery nearest us in the howe.

It marks the life of a young man who died after falling off the roof of the church, where he had climbed to witness his own father's funeral, after his boss had forbidden him time off to attend.

34. BALLAD OF SANDY MITTY

Or one man's life in fantasyland

■■■ ■■■ ■■■ ■■■

"Groups would huddle closer lest Sandy saw a gap and joined them. Elsewhere, drinks would be suddenly gulped down and clocks and watches examined closely."

IT HAS been a covinial week in the howe. I had a phone call from an acquaintance of old a few days ago. While it would be nice to say that it awoke pleasant memories, which would be true in part, it is better to be honest and admit that I was anxious throughout the call that he would tell me at any moment that he had plans to revisit his old haunts soon and that he would like to meet again.

Or, worse, that he would like to stay with us for a few days.

We'll call him Sandy, which is not his real name, for reasons that will become clear. Sandy does not live in The Press and Journal's circulation area any more and, consequently, Sandy is unlikely to fall out with me or be hurt because Sandy will not hear of the tales I am about to tell.

Like many easygoing sons of northern Scotland, Sandy is a topper. I can't deny it. He always has been. He was kind to his mother when she was alive. He helped out in his community. He was always among the first to dip into his pocket for charity events. Children and animals adored him.

But Sandy has one major fault.

Sandy tells lees.

They're not malicious lies, because he would be horrified to

147

think that anyone was suffering by his stories. Sandy's tales are more flights of fancy or tall stories. Had he been born 40 years earlier, Sandy might have been James Thurber's inspiration for Walter Mitty.

For instance, Sandy's quick thinking has prevented a fuel-tanker crash. Sandy has been in a queue in a bank in Glasgow when masked men have burst in and told everyone to lie on the floor. Sandy has faced down a mad dog, giving nearby adults a vital few moments to save the life of a terrified child.

Sandy has a second-cousin who works for Nasa. Sandy has a relative in the Home Counties who has to tell his family that he is a civil servant, when Sandy knows perfectly well that it's a cover for his real job in the senior ranks of the intelligence service. Sandy's great-grandfather was an uncredited engineering designer of the Forth Bridge. Or was it the Tay one?

Sandy's uncle in Canada once kissed Marilyn Monroe. Sandy's great-uncle clarified the ballistics theory which led to the development of the bouncing bomb. Sandy's sister was always on the point of landing a recording contract with an international record label.

I could go on, but you catch the drift. I'll be most surprised if you don't know a Sandy of your own. There are a few of them about, I hear.

No one was ever sure if Sandy believed these stories or if he simply couldn't help himself. Did he inhabit the twilight world between reality and fantasy? Had repetition made them truth to him? Or was he aware that they were stories and didn't particularly care?

In any case, they cost him many friendships. Once-staunch allies who had admired Sandy's other qualities could bear the shaggy-dog stories no longer. Their admiration turned to sufferance and then to thinly veiled derision.

It was instructive to watch Sandy's progress at a social function. Groups would huddle closer lest Sandy saw a gap and joined them. Elsewhere, drinks would be suddenly gulped down and clocks and watches examined closely. People who had arrived only 15 minutes before would remember pressing appointments.

Others would exchange knowing looks behind his back. I found it incredibly sad, and all the sadder for the fact that Sandy appeared not to realise that he was being spurned and remained as cheerful as ever.

I have never seen anyone appear to be so happy sitting on his own in a crowded room as Sandy was. I wondered often what Sandy made of his own company when he closed the door of his flat each night.

I was asked several times through the late 1970s and early 1980s why I still hadn't given Sandy the bum's rush myself. I didn't know then and I'm not entirely sure now. I suppose that the answer lies somewhere between the theory that I must be an easy mark for anything in pain and the fact that it was simpler to say nothing than to be venomous.

Sandy was harmless, in other words. He wasn't robbing pensioners. He wasn't abusing children. He wasn't defrauding his employer. He wasn't dealing in drugs or bursting gas meters. He told tall stories.

Some of the more persistent friends posited the theory that I should have been more angry with Sandy than I was. He was insulting me, they said, because clearly he supposed that I was gullible enough to believe him.

But I don't think Sandy thought that way at all, you see. It wasn't a connection he would have made because he was not a calculating person. A psychologist or psychiatrist would make a great deal of Sandy and do a far better job than I, but I think Sandy was so crippled by a sense of inferiority, insignificance and poor self-worth that his only escape was fiction.

It was just a shame that the fiction was so chronic and elaborate that it led once good friends to look on him, eventually, as inferior, insignificant and of little worth.

I wondered often if the people who so derided Sandy when he wasn't there were ever brave enough to say anything to his face even gently or jokingly. I have no room to talk because although I never made fun of him, I certainly didn't confront him, either.

But I was there when, eventually, someone did.

It was one evening at a retirement function when a much older mutual friend had listened, as I had myself, to several new Sandy tales, including something involving the Suez Canal, as I recall, when the older man put down his drink and said quietly: "Sandy, why do you tell so many lies?"

It was a question dozens of other people had asked each other, but never Sandy, for 20 years. It came so unexpectedly, so suddenly, that I froze, aghast that it had been said in front of me.

You know the feeling when a hot flash of panic and embarrassment runs like an electric charge from your neck up to your feet, up your back, and then your face turns white and, just as quickly, flushes red and roasting, all in half a second?

That was me.

I stared into my lap. I might even have closed my eyes to try to pretend it wasn't happening; I can't remember.

There was no remonstration in the older man's tone. No mockery. Most of all, there was no sympathy. It was a bare question delivered barely, with a steady gaze.

I waited for Sandy to give the answer which all of us had awaited for almost 20 years. All he did was shrug his shoulders and grin. Tall tales were not the big issue for Sandy that they were for everyone else, it seemed. Perhaps he had never really expected anyone to believe him. Perhaps he just enjoyed it.

Perhaps he was the one taking us all for mugs all along.

▬▬ ▬▬ ▬▬ ▬▬

Sandy was on the phone just a few days before this book went to press. It was reassuring to find that he hadn't changed, and seemed not in the least fazed by having been outed all those years before.

Sandy had just lost a lottery ticket which would have assured him a six-figure win.

35. HOSPITALITY OF THE HOUSE

Or how to cope with an unexpected guest

▬ ▬ ▬ ▬

*"He appeared at our front door two Saturdays ago with
little more than a suitcase, a suntan and a mouthful of
the most dazzling teeth this side of a basking shark."*

IT HAS been a transatlantic week in the howe. We have been
hosting a guest from Colorado. We were not related to him.
We did not know him. We had not met him. We had not even
spoken to him. However, for reasons which accelerated outwith
our control at a frightening rate, he appeared at our front door two
Saturdays ago with little more than a suitcase, a suntan and a
mouthful of the most dazzling teeth this side of a basking shark.

"Hi, I'm Clayton!"

Lesson One: when others are seeking accommodation for their
holiday chums, think quickly and pass the buck. On no account
hesitate, for hesitation shall be thy undoing.

Clayton from Colorado arrived as a result of someone else's ill-
advised holiday conversation. You know the thing: "You're from
the States? You've never been to Scotland? Oh, you must come
and visit Scotland some time. It's a beautiful country. You'd have
a marvellous time."

Most people of most nationalities understand the unwritten
etiquette of holiday chit-chat or, if they don't, at least wait for an
exchange of two or three letters over a year or more to allow a
more stable friendship to develop.

Not Clayton from Colorado.

He took it all horribly literally and called his instant Scots friend virtually within hours of her return from holiday to say that he had booked tickets, changed money and would be arriving six weeks later, which he hoped was convenient but it was his only "window" between fishing expeditions, ski-ing in the Rockies and cruising in the Caribbean with his mother.

For a 29-year-old, he led an active existence.

At least his instant Scots friend did the decent thing. She said how delighted she was. No, really, absolutely chuffed. Over the moon. Then she put the phone down and screamed.

After doing the rounds of likely billets, all reporting no room at the inn, and with her pleading becoming increasingly desperate and the bottom lip beginning to wobble, she turned to us.

Mr and Mrs Mug and Little Puppy Mug.

"You have plenty of room," we were advised. "It would only be for a week. And I could take a week's holiday and wheech him off to the West Coast and down to Edinburgh. I'll show him the country, as it were. Oh, please."

Maybe it's because Mrs Harper and I like Americans and know that they are exceptionally hospitable on their own soil. Or maybe we admired her willingness to put herself out for a relative stranger. Or maybe we were anxious that our nation was not let down for lack of an ambassador. In any case, evidently we didn't say: "Clear off" quickly enough.

And so Clayton from Colorado bowled up, having flown from the US to London and then to Glasgow, because he thought that that looked like the closest big airport to Aberdeen, thus requiring us to drive a 320-mile round trip to collect him.

If you have suffered jet lag, you know it is most telling after flying West to East. For at least a week, you yawn and shamble at work, and lie staring by the glow of the alarm clock at night.

Not Clayton from Colorado.

Clayton from Colorado slept only four hours a night. Clayton from Colorado was sitting in the kitchen each midnight when we retired. When we descended next morning, Clayton from Colorado was there again, with a cheery: "Hi! Sleep well?"

Mrs Harper thought he was simply charming and high-spirited. I think he might well have been made from a kit of titanium parts in a research lab in Estonia.

On Clayton's second night, we asked what of Scotland he would like to see. "Oh, gee, you got me. I don't know. Everything!"

We explained that everything in a week was a little ambitious, but would he make do with Macduff meantime? He said he would, and when he discovered that Macduff was one of Scotland's premier fishing and boatbuilding ports, he became most animated "because I got two boats myself".

We took him the long way round, weaving along highways and byways and through villages, towns and hamlets, taking almost 150 miles to do it.

Along the way, he pronounced himself peckish and wondered if we could show him some "typical Scotch cuisine". Since typical Scotch cuisine is at a premium at 10pm on a Sunday night, we had to resort to a chip shop. I won't say where, but it wasn't Macduff.

Clayton stood in the queue with us, fascinated by the hissing fat and steam, and the shuffling of scoops among birstled chips. Then the assistant, an amply upholstered matron, who clearly enjoyed her own product to excess, turned and inquired which of her wares Clayton from Colorado might like to sample.

She did so in that time-honoured way of North-east chippers: "Aye?"

"Hi, ma'am," said Clayton from Colorado. "How are you tonight?"

Realising instantly that she was in the presence of a crushingly polite and courteous colonial and wishing to reply in kind, she summoned her full ambassadorial powers, stared at him and said: "Fit?"

Clayton from Colorado had a busy week. Loch Ness. Distillery. Balmoral. Skye. Glenshee. Edinburgh. Woollen mill. Aberdeen. Stone circle. Applecross. Dufftown. By the close of his time in Scotland, he was desperate to see the inside of a Scottish pub, so his instant Scots friend, by now dead on her feet and kept awake only by uncomfortable shoes and a cattle prod, repaired with him to a saloon bar.

After a few spiced rums, they were joined by a darts team

celebrating a resounding victory in some pub league or other. Clayton from Colorado, mesmerised by all this hilarity and bonhomie; making heavy weather of the broadest of broad North-east accents, and emboldened by his sixth spiced rum, marched up, held out his hand and said: "Congratulations, guys! That sure is a trophy!" And *they* didn't know what to make of him, either.

Clayton has gone home now. He gave us all hugs, which delighted Mrs Harper, but didn't do much for me. Neither did I much care for his habit of strolling round the house in nothing but boxer shorts, showing off his lithe tanned legs, his muscular chest, his rippling biceps, broad shoulders and rigid stomach.

Some of us don't need to flaunt our exceptionally manly physiques so blatantly, I told Mrs Harper. She nodded, which meant, of course, that she was as horrified as I.

Clayton is back in Colorado, having spent a whirlwind week and having slept for, at most, a total of 17 hours and 42 minutes.

He has returned with entirely the wrong idea about Scottish weather, and is so enamoured of Caledonia, apparently, that he is considering abandoning his next year's Caribbean cruise in favour of a trip around the Hebrides.

Unfortunately, we are going away for most of next year. And probably the year after. And the year after that.

Clayton came across hoping for a Caledonian romance, but the original holiday friendship in the US had palled back on this side of the pond.

He returned to Colorado, his hormones still on the hotter. Gentleman that he was, he wrote once or twice, but presumably he has now moved on to amorous pastures new.

36. FRENCH CONNECTION

Or why you should say thank-you before it's too late

▬ ▬ ▬ ▬

"She taught French. She was a spinster; Brethren I believe,
and deferred to no pupil. Even the bad boys were worried
about her."

IT HAS been a prolational week in the howe. I was enjoying Hamish Watt's column yesterday on the 350th anniversary of his alma mater, Keith Grammar School, when one of his paragraphs struck a chord. He noted that:

"It is a pity that time rolls on and has removed so many of our teachers before we could thank them for their forbearance."

I confess that the sentiment drew me up for, several years ago, I had a similar experience, opportunity, call it what you will. I am not going to name the teacher in question, but anyone who is familiar with my alma mater and who is of roughly my vintage or older cannot fail to recognise her.

She taught French. She was a spinster; Brethren I believe, and deferred to no pupil. Even the bad boys were worried about her.

I'll admit that she frightened me. She insisted on 110% application, and shirkers or lead-swingers were of no use to her. She didn't seem to mind strugglers, for they were a challenge. I fell into the struggler category.

Anyone who was performing below ability would be invited out to the blackboard to write up a problematic sentence. The slightest mistake led to her swift descent, and a sharp powk-powk-powking on the shoulder that had the poor pupil bouncing off the blackboard and raising clouds of chalk stue. I know, for I was that pupil on at least four occasions in five years.

She had a habit of conducting a 40-question verbal exercise in desk order in the classroom. She must have known perfectly well that, throughout the class, pupils were counting down the rows and columns of desks to establish which would become their question from the book, and then begin rehearsing it like mad.

Such was her sense of mischief that she would habitually alter the sequence, jumping a desk or two or starting a row at the wrong end, thus throwing an entire class of otherwise worldly teenagers into confusion, panic and furious mental arithmetic.

And yet, if you were to ask any of us now to trot out a few impromptu phrases of French, I'm reasonably sure that they would trip from our tongues with little thought.

If any of my contemporaries or I get to reminiscing about school, you may be sure that at least one of us will say: "She was a holy terror, but she fairly taught you French."

It was the fact that she fairly taught me French that had made me consider for many years that I should write her a letter of thanks. Her work has saved my bacon in many a tight spot in French-speaking countries in the last 20 years.

But, you know how it is, I never quite got round to it. Other things always seemed to be pressing and I figured — erroneously, as Mrs Harper tells me — that teachers really don't want to be bothered with people they dispatched years before.

The event that finally sparked me into doing something came on a trip to France. I had gone down early to breakfast, but had found that everyone else in the hotel had apparently had much the same idea, for the breakfast room was filled to capacity.

I managed to find myself a seat at a table for three, occupied by one solitary Frenchman. We nodded our greetings and he swept a lazy hand at one of the seats, indicating that it was not taken. I sat down and tried to catch the waiter's attention.

I remember clearly that while the waiter filled my glass from a pitcher of orange juice, I asked (in French) for hot chocolate, some croissants and honey. That was all; no philosophical discussion or an Institute of Linguists exam.

I sat back, sipping the juice, gazing out of the window and beginning to prepare myself mentally for the day, when my dining companion leaned across and said in his native tongue: "I must congratulate you on your accent. It was just like a Frenchman. It was only towards the end that I guessed you came from England."

I didn't put him right, and I mention the exchange not to puff my ego because, notice, all he was complimenting was my accent, not my grasp of the language, which was just as well. I could easily have ordered a bicycle-pump, two socks and a hedgehog.

I mention it because that was the first time in more than 25 years of speaking French that I had been given any inkling by a native speaker as to how well I had been taught.

I mentioned the French-breakfast incident when I returned home, and Mrs Harper was adamant that I could delay no longer. She might even have stuffed notepaper under my nose and thrust the pen into my hand; I can't quite recall.

It is always difficult to open channels after two decades, but I began by conceding that she would probably not remember me, the small boy from the howe, although she had taught me French for five years from the early 1970s.

I said that I had been meaning to write thank her for her efforts and her persistence in moments when my prospects as a linguist must have seemed darker than a dark shade of midnight black.

In order that the letter wasn't too much of an exercise in creepery, I wrote honestly that hers were not the classes I had looked forward to most at the time, usually fearing sudden impact with the blackboard, but that, on reflection, hers were the classes that had the most beneficial, practical and protracted results.

Then I outlined the incident in France which had prompted me to write and ascribed it wholly to her efforts, which was the truth.

There was no reply.

I would like to claim that I had not really expected a reply, but I would be lying. I riffled through the post for a couple of weeks, hoping for just a note of acknowledgement. There was nothing.

Weeks passed.

Months.

Periodically, I would wonder if I had offended her by saying that I had not looked forward to her lessons. Occasionally, I will admit, I cursed myself quietly for having been so forward as to write to someone I had not troubled for more than 20 years.

Then, a week before a Christmas, came a small Christmas card. Inside was folded a single sheet of airmail paper. I recognised the handwriting at once. It was the same hand which, in red ink throughout the early Seventies, had declared: "No! No! No! Must do better! You expect to be spoon-fed!"

It was more faint and feathery than I remembered, but the elegant looping of the script was as before. She was gracious enough to thank me and apologise for taking so long to reply, but said she couldn't let Christmas go by without getting in touch.

She was not effusive (she had little reason to be), but she recalled incidents as she had tried to hammer irregular verbs into me and concluded by saying that she was always pleased to hear from anyone who felt that her work had been of benefit.

I must have been beaming when I put down the letter, for Mrs Harper had adopted one of her and-what-did-I-tell-you? looks.

Literally weeks later, I was scanning The Press and Journal and read that my French teacher had passed away peacefully.

I was shocked, of course; a little sad, but overwhelmingly relieved that I had finally shifted myself to drop her a line after 20 years just to let her know that I appreciated the results of all her efforts and that she hadn't entirely wasted her time with me.

Her untimely death is why I always urge anyone who cannot get round to writing a thank-you letter, or just to saying thank you to anyone who has helped in the past, to stir himself and do it.

You never know when it might be too late.

I should have named her and been done with it.
Everyone guessed. Her name was Sheila Craig.

37. QUEEN OF THE CLEANERS

Or why you'll find philosophy where you least expect it

▬ ▬ ▬ ▬

"She was not a pretty woman. Not even Elsie would claim
that she was clubbie-book material. She was 5ft and had a
46-46-46 figure, clad in a pink bri-nylon overall."

IT HAS been a hygiologous week in the howe. For reasons we needn't explore here, I had to be in the Aberdeen Journals building one morning last week, in that limbo 90 minutes between the last Press and Journal light being switched off and the first Evening Express light being switched on.

At that time, the visitor meets only the stern gaze of the security chaps, the automatic floodlights and the alarm sensors. No colleagues. No visitors. No appointments. No phones ringing. No yatter and chatter. Bliss. Productive bliss, too.

There's a freedom to working with no one else around: a freedom that is normally the preserve of the cleaners.

Which brings us to a lesson for every young executive; one that no business school teaches but which is the bedrock to a successful corporate career.

Never underestimate the cleaners.

If cleaners wanted, they could clip your wings most spectacularly. Never take them for granted. For a few hours, even the highest-powered boardroom in the most exalted headquarters of any organisation, business or government ministry becomes the bailiwick of the cleaners. They rule supreme. Directors' diktats at 4pm are supplanted by the might of the mop and the clout of the cloot by 4am. Where the board members puff cigars, the cleaners puff Vim, and the Vim is a lot more useful.

The cleaner has a luxury and power that few other employees enjoy, for she can storm about, muttering dark mutterings about those-who-inhabit-the-floor-where-the-carpet-is-deep, confident that nothing will come of it for no one can hear. How she carries out her duties can affect the entire operation of an organisation for the following 24 hours.

If that's not power, what is?

The most characterful cleaner that I ever knew was Elsie. Elsie was an urban philosopher in her late 40s, responsible for the hygiene and order of the training centre where I learned my craft in the mid-1970s.

I have tried to recall Elsie's second name, but I can't; for as long as we knew her, Elsie was just Elsie, or Elsie the Cleaner when she demanded the respect that was her due.

She was not a pretty woman. Not even Elsie would claim that she was clubbie-book material. She was barely 5ft and had a 46-46-46 figure, clad in a pink bri-nylon overall and topped by a flare of wiry, grey-black hair.

Her arms were red and leathery from decades of buckets of Flash. (Elsie scorned rubber gloves, She claimed that rubber spoiled the feel a professional cleaner got for how clean something was.)

A dog-end dangled permanently from the corner of her mouth and, now that I think about it, I can't recall having seen her light up or stub one out. For as long as I knew her, that fag-end was always an inch long and listing to starboard at 45 degrees.

For all the visual nightmare that Elsie was, she sailed up and down the corridors with all the majesty and presence of the Queen Mary. You knew when Elsie was in the building. People stepped aside for Elsie. People held open doors for Elsie. People *liked* Elsie.

When she spoke, she spoke in a strong Geordie accent, made baritone by 40 years of smoking. The accent was fine for those of us who came from north of Leeds, but the ones from south of Watford struggled mightily to catch the strangled vowels, and Elsie had very little time for them. She refused to soften her accent for anyone, which was admirable.

Sartorially, she deferred to no one. Elsie preferred to wear soft-soled pom-pom slippers while on duty because, she said, they helped polish the floor and were less hard on her bunion.

Unfortunately, her slippers were the sort of pastel-pink, fluffy boudoir efforts that Jean Harlow might have worn before slipping between silk sheets.

They were as dainty as the rest of her was sturdy, and the effect as she tramped down a corridor was comic, although not one of us would dared have grinned in her presence; Elsie looked as if she could take care of herself.

Indeed, Elsie looked as if she had taken care of herself on several occasions already. A tough childhood on the Depression streets of South Shields must have hardened anyone.

It was late one March evening that Elsie popped her head round the door of the lecture room. I was alone, working late on a newspaper-law exercise, and she had not expected to find anyone in.

She apologised for disturbing me and hoped I wouldn't mind if she did "some dusting and that". But "some dusting and that" became a conversation, and although my books were open, my attention soon belonged to Elsie who, dusting furiously, treated me to her life's views.

"I work for an agency, pet," she told me. "They pay us bugger aal, like, but it's regular money and that's what matters, isn't it?

"I'm better off than most of the girls. Most of the girls get put a fortnight here and a fortnight there and they never get to know a place. They never get a feel for a place and what it needs to keep it clean.

"I've been here for eight years and I'm on top of the job. There's nobody can say that I'm not, can they now?"

I shook my head in agreement and she paused to look round the room with pride. Where I saw just another room, she saw difficult nooks and corners, ledges prone to gathering dust and windows that showed the smears when the sunlight landed in a particular way.

"On top of the job, that's the secret," she said, beginning dusting again. "I'll tell you something else. The other girls never get to know people because the people don't get to know them. To the bosses in the office buildings the other girls clean, they're just cleaners.

"The bosses march past in their suits and they look the other road. Or sometimes they look at the girls and they're looking as if they've stood in something. And these are laddies looking at women old enough to be their mothers, sometimes even their grandmothers. Don't tell me it doesn't happen, because I've seen it.

"Only it's never happened to me, you see, because I speak to them. If you speak to someone, they have to speak back to you. One night, it'll maybe be just a 'goodnight', but it's a start.

"You have to make them speak to you, and that way they get to know you and you get to know them. That way, you're not just the cleaner or something that blew in in the middle of the night."

She stopped and there was a look of pride in her face. "And that's why I'm not the cleaner here, pet; I'm Elsie."

It is a lesson I have never forgotten. It is a lesson many more people have still to learn.

Elsie must be around 70 now, and out to pasture. I hope a lifetime of Vim, Flash, Mr Sheen and Mr Bloo won't have spoiled a happy retirement. I imagine she's still wielding that mop vigorously in her own home somewhere in Byker or Wallsend.

As for our own cleaners at the Press and Journal, they're gems, although I daren't tell of the day the Scottish Secretary visited the newsroom in 1978.

38. BUMPING THOSE GUMS

Or why you need to be a saint to deal with public devils

▬ ▬ ▬ ▬

"He sighed pointedly; craned forward to scowl at other
people's luggage, and turned to the queue behind to show
others what an irate chap he was."

IT HAS been a threnodial week in the howe. I met the woman who is in charge of promoting Aberdeen worldwide. Not Aberdeen, Scotland. Aberdeen, Washington. Linda Spalding is her name, and she was on a quick tour of Scotland with several dozen other representatives from the Pacific North-west of the US.

The American states of Washington and Oregon, and the Canadian province of British Columbia have banded together to call themselves Cascadia. It's a tourism marketing exercise named after the Cascade Mountains which are the backbone of that part of North America.

Cascadia had realised that the strong pound and weak yen made it imperative to try to tempt more British tourists to this land of clean mountain air, pine-clad hills, apple orchards, tulip fields, whale-watching, whitewater rafting, Frasier and Microsoft.

I appreciated the invitation to dinner, because I'm a big fan of Washington, Oregon and BC. The CO and I have returned several times to the Pacific North-west since I started going there in my bachelor days in the 1980s, and have become good friends with B.J. Stokey, who looks after Seattle worldwide. Seattle was the CO's first taste of the US and it hooked her for life.

But last week was the first time I had met Linda, and we were able to empathise about tourist problems. I explained the difficulties facing our Aberdeen in tempting foreign tourists out of the well-worn route between Edinburgh and the Highlands. Her difficulty is persuading visitors not to stay in Seattle for their whole holiday, but to strike out to rural and coastal Washington.

One of Linda's fellow-travellers, Billie, from the Oregon Tourism Commission, was something of a conversation piece in the assembly. British Airways had lost Billie's luggage on the direct flight from Seattle to Heathrow, and she had had to make several presentations and attend several receptions wearing the clothes in which she had travelled.

"Did you complain?" I asked.

"No," said Billie. "They don't do these things deliberately. It's an accident, and they fixed it real quick. Why complain? They're doing everything they can. Complaining doesn't speed them up."

"That's a very unusual attitude," I said.

"It's too unusual," agreed Linda. "Before I worked for Aberdeen, I was a complaints consultant for seven years. I worked out company strategies. I told employees how far they could go and what promises they couldn't make.

"Believe me, the customer who understands that problems happen to anyone and that the company will repair matters just as soon as it can usually gets the problem solved much more quickly than the person who blows off steam at an innocent employee."

To prove her case, Linda told of standing at a check-in queue at a major US airport late last year. The queue was barely inching towards the counter; the airline's computers were down and check-in procedure had slowed to a crawl. The man in front of Linda had been growing increasingly more irate with lack of progress.

Linda could tell he was not a model of tolerance by the way he sighed pointedly; craned forward to scowl at other people's luggage; rocked impatiently from one foot to the other, and turned to the queue behind to show others what an irate chap he was.

Eventually, he reached the top of the queue and slung two suitcases on to the check-in scales. Linda said that what followed was an abysmal display of staff abuse by a customer.

"I have been standing here for half an hour," he said. "Your airline stinks." The check-in woman took his ticket and began tapping keys on her computer.

"Did you hear me? Your airline stinks. You treat us all like cattle."

"Sir," said the check-in woman, "we are having sporadic problems with our computers. I appreciate the fact that you have been waiting for longer than you would like and I apologise."

"You apologise. You apologise? That's it? An apology? You think that's enough? I want an upgrade to business class."

"Sir, I cannot do that. Business class is absolutely full today."

"First class, then."

"I cannot upgrade you through two fare levels. You are travelling on a coach [economy] ticket. I could upgrade you as far as Business Class in exceptional circumstances but, as I have told you already, Business Class is full today and I cannot change that."

"Lady, all I hear is what you cannot do. You cannot do this. You cannot do that. What can you do? Anything at all? Or are you just stupid?"

"Sir, I thank you for your patience with me. You're quite right; I'm stupid. Now, if you'll bear with me, I'm going to have to do a manual check-in; the computer is still down."

"Doesn't this pig's-behind airline train you people to work a little faster? Don't you have a back-up computer?"

"Sir, I'm working at the limit of my training. I'm doing everything I can but, I guess you're right, it's just not enough. I don't even know why they keep me here."

"Hot dang, you're dealing with the public, girlie. We pay your wages. We want service. I want value for my money."

"And I'm letting you down at every turn. I'm just not good enough for you. In fact, I'm not fit to speak to any customers." She slid a boarding pass and the ticket stub back across the counter to the man. "But we thank you for your patience and I thank you for tolerating me. Have a nice day."

The man snorted his last little indignant snort, picked up his briefcase and stormed off to the departure gate.

Linda stepped forward and placed her ticket on the counter

"You know," she said. "I've worked in complaint handling for seven years. I've run complaints departments. I've developed corporate policies for complaint handling, but I've very rarely seen an employee handle an irate customer as well as you did now."

"You think so?"

"Certainly, I do. Most people take complaints personally, but you didn't, although he was so terribly rude to you. Even I would have found it difficult. How do you manage?"

"Well, you know," said the check-in woman, "I used to take it personally. I took it personally for years. I used to go home at night and replay difficult customers in my head. And I would get more and more tense, and I couldn't sleep and I wasn't eating. And it wasn't doing me any good at all."

"Then I had counselling and I learned that angry customers are not angry with me; they're angry with the circumstances. If the complaint is genuine and you let them see you empathise, even if there's nothing you can do to make it better, it's less stressful."

"Well, congratulations," said Linda, taking her boarding pass and ticket stub. "Keep up the good work."

"And besides," said the check-in woman; "he's going to London and his bags are going to Japan."

These are the stories of oneupmanship that readers of The Press and Journal seem to like. I don't know why they take vicarious pleasure in seeing pompous blighters cut down to size, but they do.

I sent off a cutting of the column to Linda, hoping for an update of how the angry customer replied, but she didn't know.

I imagine he wasn't best chuffed.

39. HEELS ON WHEELS

Or how to spot a driver from northern Scotland

■■ ■■ ■■ ■■

*"Jimmy must have reasoned, presumably, that there was
no need to bother with any of the other gears until the first
one had worn out."*

IT HAS been an impavid week in the howe. I have been doing
what seems to have been a lot of long-distance driving lately;
not that I mind, for I have always liked driving, but it seems
to be becoming more tiring, or more tedious, or both.

Engineers and designers have spent millions upon millions of
pounds, marks and yen on research and development to make
sure that cars are easy to drive. Trunk roads have been dualled
and straightened to move traffic as quickly and safely as possible
— a gold-seal achievement for travel efficiency, but death to
interesting and enjoyable driving.

So I have been noticing how other drivers relieve the boredom
of the 70mph drone, and it has nothing to do with keeping their
minds on the road ahead. Some have been on their mobiles. Some
have been catching up on their shaving. Some have been leafing
through clipboards of papers.

Some colleagues and acquaintances have told me that they
practise mental arithmetic. Some dream of their eight Desert Island
Discs. Others put together their perfect menu.

There must be safer ways to tackle high-speed boredom.

You could always do what one of my contemporaries on
another Scottish newspaper did a couple of summers ago in

London. Her experience cured her of carbound boredom for all time.

She had to get from Kings Cross to Waterloo in a hurry and decided to hop into a taxi, rather than risk getting lost on the Underground. "I'd always wanted to tell a taxi-driver to 'step on it and there'll be an extra fiver in it for you'," she said. "So that's what I did."

She regretted her daring within the first quarter-mile. The taxi-driver took off as if demons were grasping at his bumper. He hared along narrow alleys, burst into queues of traffic, clipped kerbs, jinked from lane to lane, ran amber lights, cut up other drivers and more or less left a swathe of shaking fists, spluttering faces and tooting horns wherever he went.

"I was rolling from side to side in the back of the taxi," said his passenger, "trying hard not to be sick and wondering if saying something would upset his professional pride. I kept telling myself that he was only doing what I had asked, but I can tell you that I was really, really scared. We were missing accidents by fractions of a second."

The journey was successful, however, and she reached Waterloo with fully 10 minutes to spare. As she stepped out and leaned into the passenger window to pay off the driver, she must have looked dishevelled and deathly pale, because the driver beamed and said in broad, chirpy Cockney: "'Ope you wasn't scared, darlin."

"Well," she said, "there was once or twice I thought we would crash so, yes, I was a little nervous with all that speed."

"Nah," he said, pocketing the cash. "Do what I do. Close your eyes."

That taxi-driver would have found kindred spirits in many rural North-east drivers of yore, many of whose exploits are legendary. These were the men (remarkably few women) who spoke with pride of never having passed a driving test in their lives and, frankly, it showed.

One of the most biting, albeit good-humoured views came in the late 1980s in a letter from Falkirk to the Readers' Questions spot in the Press and Journal Saturday motoring page.

To the best of my recollection, the writer was a commercial traveller, well used to the different driving styles across the country, and he asked something like: "Can any of your readers explain to me that peculiar phenomenon, apparently exclusive to North-east Scotland, by which the wearing of a flat cap or bonnet by the driver reduces the maximum speed of any vehicle to 35mph, and to 15mph if a field of cattle is in the vicinity?"

No reader did, but I don't doubt that a few will have been smiling.

Jimmy was one such bunneted driver. I barely remember him from my teenage years, save for his wonderfully loose interpretation of what constituted driving. Even as a 14-year-old, I would stop and marvel at Jimmy's ability to make maximum use of first gear. He must have reasoned, presumably, that there was no need to bother with any of the others until the first one had worn out.

Consequently, the roads round the Garioch would fill daily with the scream of an engine longing to explode; heads would turn and, presently, Jimmy's car would round the bend in the centre of the town at a sedate 11mph. Jimmy had style.

I enjoyed Jimmy's insistence on making full use of both sides of the road, irrespective of oncoming traffic. I admired his parking panache, in which the kerb and the side of his car had only a passing acquaintance, and the vehicle's tail protruded jauntily towards the centre of the street.

I admired his stubborn refusal to use indicators, or even hand signals, and I remember one of Jimmy's neighbours explaining that Jimmy was worried that excessive use of the indicators would flatten the battery, and that hand signals were out of the question because "I'm aye lang by the corner afore I get the windae doon".

Nothing to do with cars, but it was Jimmy who passed into Garioch lore in the 1940s, I believe, for his cool in a crisis. Nothing fazed Jimmy, and admiring tales are told still of his level-headedness. Jimmy kept a calm sooch.

His language was also somewhat ripe but, as is often the case out in the country, there was no malice in it so no one took offence.

That free tongue means that very few Jimmy anecdotes are printable, save for one.

Jimmy's house went on fire one night in the early 1950s. By the time the fire brigade arrived, there was very little to be done. The men played a couple of hoses into the roar of the flames, but it was clear even before they began that the hoosie would soon be nothing but ashes and charred timbers.

Other men might have raged or been overcome with emotion. Not Jimmy.

Jimmy studied the flames as they enveloped his home. Whatever he was thinking, no one knew, for there was nary a flicker across his face. He began fumbling in his jaicket pooch for his packet of Woodbines and pulled one out.

He picked up a small, smouldering stick that had billowed out from the heat of the blaze and had fallen near his feet.

The story goes that he lit the cigarette with the burning stick and then tossed the stick back towards the flames.

When he stepped back, he realised that a little knot of his neighbours had been watching him.

"Aye," he said, acknowledging them, "at least I'm still gettin the gweed o ma hoose."

The mailbag after this column contained a number of stories designed, I suspect, to redress the balance in men's favour.

Among them was a tale from a garage mechanic who sold a pint of oil to a young woman driver and noticed she was still under her car's bonnet 20 minutes later. When he investigated, he found she was pouring the oil down the dipstick hole.

40. PLAYING THE RACE CARD

Or why reading between the lines would help

━━━ ━━━ ━━━ ━━━

*"We need to draw the important distinction between
genuine racism and that brand of 'racism' which is
claimed by anyone who can't get on with other people."*

IT HAS been a discordant week in the howe. I have been
swithering for some weeks now about mentioning this at all,
but it is so important to so many people, not just to me, that
ignoring it is past being an option.

If you have been following the regional news, you will know
that Portknockie, that pearl of the Banffshire coast, has found itself
unwittingly in the media for the second time in two years because
a family has accused elements in the rest of the village of racism.

Portknockie has been hurt deeply by the claim and many
Banffshire people have rushed to defend its reputation as a
perfectly normal, civil and peaceable North-east community. I can
empathise with their astonishment and understand the distress this
must have caused, because no small village likes the torch of
national attention shone on it for such unfortunate reasons.

I empathise because now another North-east community has
been accused of racism, open as well as covert, by two families.
That community is my own. The howe.

It's not my business, nor is it the business of the Press and
Journal, to endorse or dismiss the detail of individuals'
experiences and grievances, but it is certainly pertinent to pose a
question or two. You'll forgive the vested interest.

Principally, I find it curious that the howe apparently has turned racist so quickly; not only quickly, but with such stealth that it went unnoticed by everyone in the place.

I find it curious because within a 15-mile radius of my house are at least three farms which are, or were, run by Polish men for more than 40 years. They came because they liked the place, liked the people, married here and stayed here. They were regarded highly as friends, neighbours and good people.

I know of not a single incident of abuse that they might have suffered, and I doubt that my elders and betters could recall one either.

One farm was run by many years by a former German PoW (who is now an accomplished Doric-speaker). If this were inherently a racist place, that racism would have shown itself at its ugliest in the immediate post-war years, when indigenous families were coming to terms with the loss of loved ones in the war.

There was nothing.

Italians who were imprisoned at the PoW camp nine miles down the road return year after year — albeit the numbers are diminishing — to keep up 50-year friendships. Many are on first-name terms with their Scottish counterparts who were captured and imprisoned in the wartime invasion of Italy.

In the Sixties, the howe provided trade for a succession of Indian and Pakistani tradesmen from Aberdeen. The one I recall alighted from the bus every Wednesday and marched round the village with his brown suitcase of wares.

Had this been a racist community, he would have met a succession of closed doors and twitching net curtains. Instead, to my certain knowledge, he was welcomed into homes and plied with fly cups to such a degree that it was often touch and go whether or not he would catch the bus home.

If this were inherently a racist community, the Korean family who lived among us for several years would have barricaded themselves into their home. As it was, they developed a warm and respectful relationship with their neighbours and within the village and I know that there were tears on both sides of the garden fence when the time came to leave.

A black family has wowed the village with good humour and a willingness to get along with as many people as possible. I hope they won't be embarrassed if I say that the man of the house is one of the most popular teachers at the academy and is regarded with great respect and affection by his staunchest champions, the howe's youngsters.

I mention all this because, in context, it makes the current accusations of racism all the more astonishing and, frankly, all the more unpalatable.

Stressing now that I am discussing racism in general, and not the specifics of the cases at Portknockie and in the howe, we need to draw the important distinction between genuine racism and that increasingly prevalent brand of "racism" which is claimed by anyone who finds it difficult to get along with other people. Skin colour and country of origin have nothing to do with it.

Genuine racism, in which the catalyst is nothing more than the person's skin colour or country of origin, is deplorable and has no place in any community of any outlook. Words or acts which are calculated to hurt or injure remain one of the cruellest crimes one person can perpetrate against another. Because it arises almost always without provocation, the victim has no ready defence, which compounds the cruelty. Such racism must be punished.

But the currency is being diminished. In the way that, for many years, one could barely disagree with a Jewish person without being denounced as anti-Semitic, "racism" is being cried by too many who feel miffed or who find that the majority are not inclined to indulge them.

If that has become the qualification for racism, I, and almost everyone else, suffer it seven days a week.

Consider what a minefield such a weak definition opens up. Consider the eggshells which would have to be trod if every minor disagreement and major upset with any non-local was deemed to be racism.

Let us suppose that a Bulgarian family moved into the North-east village of Lossieburgh. Let us suppose that the man was an accomplished mechanic and took over the village garage. Let us suppose that the clientele took all their trade to him until, one day, someone turned up to collect his car after repair and found, through oversight, that he was 4p short in the cash he was carrying. Let us suppose that the Bulgarian impounded the car until the man was able to pay in full, and let us suppose that the car-owner was so incensed at such pettiness that he gave the Bulgarian a piece of his mind in particularly virulent terms and that the argument escalated until, in utter frustration, the car-owner's parting shot was: "Och, awa back tae Bulgaria."

Is that racism?

Or consider a family from Paraguay who move into Lossieburgh and one of whom causes such upset and vandalism that most of the neighbours are appalled and wish quietly that they would go.

Is that passive racism?

If the Bulgarians and the Paraguayans suddenly find that they are at the centre of ever more arguments and ever more of the spats and fallings-out which, frankly, are part and parcel of every North-east family, village and town, irrespective of the parties' colour, is that racism?

No on all three counts. That's my view. The litmus test is perfectly simple: if the person who is suffering abuse would have suffered the same abuse had he behaved in the same way and had he been born and brought up in the area, he is not suffering racism.

He is getting the same well-deserved kick up the shirt that would have been meted out to any local whose behaviour had finally exasperated too many people.

I happened to attend a community Millennium function at Portknockie not so long ago. If that's an unwelcoming village I'm a cheese sandwich.

41. SCENT OF THE COUNTRYSIDE

Or why the answer, my friend, is blowing in the wind

▬ ▬ ▬ ▬

"The sitooterie at my aunt and uncle's farm would have been typical, with a wooden bench seat polished glassy smooth by generations of assorted docks."

IT HAS been an irriguous week in the howe. Many are the joys of living in the country. Two or three times a day, we have a pair of RAF jets rattling our lums now that we are directly under the Lossie/Kinloss flightpath.

They have to fly somewhere, of course, because it would be an awful waste of money to buy all that machinery and just admire it in the hangars.

Some people complain that they fly too low and that they are very community-unfriendly because of it, but Mrs Harper and I reject the charge completely.

We have developed a warm relationship with the pilot with the ginger moustache, the bad breath and the pimple on the end of his nose, who gives us a cheery wave if either of us happens to be out with the washing.

Another joy of country life is not having streetlights. I know plenty of people campaign to have streetlights anywhere and everywhere, on the grounds that streetlights discourage housebreakers (what goes wrong in Aberdeen, then?), but I'm delighted that we are bereft here because we see the night sky more clearly without all that light pollution, that so afflicts cities.

During the recent alleged meteor shower, we knew that it was a waste of time so much more quickly than did Aberdonians, who were fretting about missing a free show, and we were able to cosy down by the fireside and read our books, perfectly content.

We are also quite delighted with all the usual country things: the fresh air, quiet, views, newsing over a fence, scope for walks and so on.

But septic tanks?

Septic tanks are normally marvellous things; a tribute to human ingenuity and so much more fragrant than the dry outside lavvies that were common to many farmhouses until as late as 30 or 40 years ago.

The sitooterie at my aunt and uncle's farm in the early 1960s would have been typical, with a wooden bench seat polished glassy smooth by generations of assorted docks, and squares of the Weekly News strung on a nail behind the door. The Press and Journal was too revered and the People's Friend too shiny.

I recall as a small boy being confused that there were two identical holes side by side in the bench and remember wondering at the communal habits of farmers, but now I know better.

Septic tanks are de rigueur in the country nowadays. Almost everyone out of reach of mains sewerage has one buried on their land and, normally, these work effectively.

What problems there are arise usually because of human error. Some people who are unaccustomed to septic tanks suffer a moment's madness or forgetfulness and pour bleach, caustic soda or other microbe-killing chemicals down the loo or kitchen sink and stop the bacteriological process stone dead.

That necessitates a speedy and plaintive call to the council to arrange a visit by the emptying lorry (known in the trade, I believe, as the honey wagon).

But it seems that septic tanks are causing problems throughout the north and North-east at the moment, and it has nothing to do with Domestos, Parozone or Mr Bloo.

We had been noticing for several months that our sinks were clearing a little more slowly than usual and that the loos were taking an extra few seconds to settle down post-flush.

I assumed that we had a minor blockage somewhere; that perhaps our visiting nephews had been passing the time flushing away fistfuls of toilet roll, as small boys do when bored.

Mrs Harper, who is much more judgmental, decided at once that I had put turps, thinners, battery acid, oven-cleaner, or something equally unpleasant — Sunny Delight, perhaps — down a sink, and she set about making her displeasure clear.

So I sought unofficial advice from a friendly plumber and his verdict was instant. Yes, it could be a blockage, he said, but it's more likely just the weather.

Apparently, Scotland is so sodden after more than a year of near-constant rain, that even industrial-sized soakaways and monster septic tanks are having problems coping with the sheer volume of water that is dormant in the ground.

It shouldn't be much of a problem for most people, he said, but people whose houses were on clay soil might notice it a little more than others. The same would go for people who lived on slopes, particularly those that ended in burns or rivers.

We live on clay soil on a slope down to a burn.

The litmus test, apparently, was to have the pipes professionally blasted by an industrial-strength pressure-washer and then to have the septic tank emptied.

Checking carefully that Mrs Harper was not aboard one of the facilities upstairs, I bade the pressure-jet man do his best.

I may tell you that the most fearful rumbling sound seemed to emanate from the depths of the earth and I half-feared for the slates, but after several minutes of whooshing, grinding and thundering, the likes of which the howe has not heard before, the pressure-jet man pronounced our tubes, caps and U-bends in fine fettle.

"It wasn't a blockage," he said.

So that was when we called in the honey wagon.

There is something mildly embarrassing about having the honey wagon roll up to your front door. Car drivers slow down as they pass, pointing it out to their passengers and having animated conversations.

The two council gentlemen who arrived, I hope with permanent head colds, seemed quite unabashed as they manoeuvred their truck up to the tank lid and set about swinging out the biggest hoover you have ever seen.

I won't describe the noises that rang around the northern edge of the howe for the following 20 minutes. I certainly won't even attempt to convey the perfume. Let's just say that the dog thought all his Christmases had arrived. He didn't know where to run first.

The upshot is that the tank was half-way to filling again within three days of being emptied; this time with clean water seeping through from the ground.

Our plumbing friend diagnosed the problem over the phone. "It's happening to just about everyone," he said. "Septic tanks are normally supposed to disperse the liquids out to dry ground, but when the ground is saturated they act like sponges instead and draw in the water. Your soakaways are finding it a challenge at the moment.

"The more clay in your soil, and the more persistent the rain, the more you'll have to live with it. There's no health hazard. It's just a nuisance."

Not half as much of a nuisance as the aroma that hung about the place for hours when visitors were due.

Although we did wonder what one of the visitors imagined the problem was when she asked discreetly if it might be possible to open a window.

Sure enough, when the drier weather came the plumbing system settled down and our ablutory network was restored to the finest of fine fettle.

Given the usual nature of a Scottish winter (or summer), however, we might have to set out contingency plans very soon.

42. SICK TO THE BACK TEETH

Or why not to trust foreign omelettes

▬ ▬ ▬ ▬

*"I could feel that familiar nausea creeping around in the
pit of my stomach and up to my throat. The man across
the aisle leaned over and asked if I was feeling all right."*

IT HAS been a crepitative week in the howe. You'll have
noticed all the fuss these last 10 days about food-poisoning.
You can hardly turn on the TV without Edwina Currie
appearing to talk about eggs, health inspections and antibiotics.

Mrs Currie is making the most of her new celebrity as a media
pundit by harking back to that minute of notoriety in 1989 when
she declared on the national television news that virtually all of
the United Kingdom's egg production was infected with
salmonella.

If you'll pardon the observation, she caused an awful stink. Egg-
producers would have put out contracts on the woman if they
could have, and there was always the suspicion that no one at
Westminster would have tried to stop them.

For Mrs Currie, TV and radio are the ideal vehicles to help her
justify her boldness 10 years ago. They also let her capitalise on
the growing impression in politics, the public and food science
that, whatever the fury of egg-producers then, she was right all the
time.

The arguments about food safety, and the fine balance among
industry jobs, public health and producer profits are not for
arguing here. Our Farm Journal pages have aired these problems

many a Saturday, and you'll have explored that already if you're interested at all.

Instead, I want to explain what food-poisoning is like from the victim's point of view. Many of you will know already, but some of you, I suspect, might be as cocky and dismissive as I used to be.

For instance, I can remember a week in the early 1980s when the Prince of Wales called off a week of engagements because of a salmonella infection. I was genuinely astonished that anyone who called himself a man would allow an upset stomach to get in the way of his work. We all feel a bit queasy from time to time, I told colleagues, but we don't all collapse in a heap and take to our beds.

Those were gentler times, when few deaths were attributed publicly to food-poisoning, and certainly caused little of the outrage and political furore that built up subsequently through the 1990s.

My view of food-poisoning malingerers, which would have done credit to a stalag commandant, did not soften for another 10 or 12 years. Then came June 21, 1996.

It was a Friday. I had been in northern France, driving towards Calais to catch the Eurostar and get myself and the car back to the UK. With a couple of hours in hand, I nipped into Le Touquet, one-time pearl of the minor English aristocracy, to see what I could see and to have myself a snack.

What's worthwhile in Le Touquet is quite compact; the place has an air of faded elegance which is attractive, but not especially enervating.

So I found myself a hotel — I think it was the Angleterre — and asked to see a café menu. It was all most enticing but, with a drive to Gatwick ahead of me and then a flight to Aberdeen, I knew that I wouldn't manage to scale a full three-course repast, so I did what I normally do and asked if they could do a quick vegetarian dish. These are usually light and tasty at the same time, which was all I wanted.

The thing about the French is that, for all their culinary flair, the veggie concept floors them every time. They just can't crack it.

Every vegetarian I know swears that the world's worst vegetarian food is created in France (the best, I'm told, is the UK's). France trots out either a boiled mush of the vegetables which were cooking anyway, or an omelette.

I got an omelette.

I'm not used to eating eggs in any blatant form. I don't care for the taste. I have never liked them. I don't like them now. And I very much doubt that I will like them any better at any point in the future.

However, the waiter returned with a flourish and put such a stupendously presented omelette in front of me that I didn't like to decline.

I began cutting off small pieces and nibbling. I'll admit that the aftertaste was odd but, being an egg novice, I assumed that that was either the way eggs tasted when they had been omeletted, or else it was perhaps something in the oil or in the spices that chef had used.

Anyway, I called a halt half-way through, paid the bill and headed for the car.

I was fine for the next three or four hours. But then, just as the stewardess came with a British Airways snack and plonked it in front of me somewhere at 35,000ft over Daventry, it was as if someone had flicked a switch in my head.

A sheen of sweat appeared on my brow. The pattern on the seatback in front of me lost its horizontal hold. I could feel that familiar nausea creeping around in the pit of my stomach and up to the back of my throat. The man across the aisle leaned over and asked if I was feeling all right, because I had turned a ghastly white.

I assumed it was airsickness, although I had never been troubled by it before. Twenty minutes later, I seemed to recover enough to tell the stewardess that I wasn't able for the meal and, no, I didn't want a drink from the bar, or any tea or coffee.

As I stood by the luggage carousel at Aberdeen Airport, bag of Duty Free in hand, the nausea began again. Only, this time, it was industrial-strength nausea — the really vicious, leaden stuff — as if someone had pumped my stomach full of month-old pond sludge and was daring me to keep it down. At one stage, the bag of Duty Free slipped from hand, the palm was so sweaty, and clinked on the floor so noisily that almost everyone in the terminal building looked round.

I had to find a seat to collect myself. It took fully 20 minutes for me to regain enough of my composure to be fit to drive.

Alas, what is normally a 40-minute drive home to the howe took nearly two hours. I stopped in every lay-by and most farm road-ends to retch and vomit. There is no dignity in public sickness.

By the time I got home and wired into the computer system to compose and deliver that evening's work down the line to HQ (what do you mean, The Press and Journal would surely be more compassionate than that?), I was in no fit state to write anything.

The stomach cramps were the worst. I was almost in tears with pain. Imagine two teams of rugby-players trotting past every 20 minutes and every last one of them, even the stupid-looking ones with bandages round their heads, kicking your midriff and enjoying it. Well, it was 50 times worse than that. Half-way between each 20-minute kicking, there was another bout of retching, long past the stage when I had nothing left to give.

I felt freezing, yet I had a temperature of 103F. Mrs Harper appeared periodically with a cold flannel and I was convinced, in my delirium, that the woman was trying to dispatch me.

Ultimately, she called in the doctor, defying my strict instructions. He arrived, did a quick examination and said that if the sickness persisted for another hour, I would be heading for hospital; no arguments.

He prepared an injection and then, in a touching and genteel gesture, asked if Mrs Harper would like to leave the room before he bared my behind.

"No," she said. "It was scary the first time I saw it, but I'm past being shocked now." The sedative worked within two hours. I slept for fully 14 hours and awoke with a thumping headache, a burning hunger and such a raging thirst that I would have ripped the legs off the first cyclist to bowl past the gate.

I didn't, of course.

Well, you never know where they've been.

43. MYSTERY OF YOUTH

Or why general knowledge is a dying art

▬ ▬ ▬ ▬

"We're not talking nuclear physics or brain surgery here:
just the stuff that used to be called general knowledge and
was tested to destruction twice a week in my day."

IT HAS been a sciolistic week in the howe. I have been wondering for several weeks about whether or not to explore today's subject at all, because it might offend many parents and, more important, their offspring.

But here goes: evidence is mounting that the modern Scottish teenager is fundamentally ignorant.

It's a shameful generalisation, I know, and I apologise to all non-thick teenagers out there, but the fact remains that a good, basic grounding on a broad range of everyday topics appears to be escaping more and more young people.

We're not talking nuclear physics or brain surgery here: just the basics; the stuff that used to be called general knowledge and which was tested to destruction on at least two primary-school afternoons a week in my day.

What is the capital of Greece? When was the Battle of Bannockburn? What was Elgar's first name?

They're of no great import in themselves, I suppose, but knowing such facts and thousands of others rounds you out and gives you a foundation for so much else, even if it's only slouching in front of the TV and shouting abuse at dense quiz-show contestants.

"Who wrote Wuthering Heights?" asked Chris Tarrant on Who Wants To Be A Millionaire? recently.

"Jane Eyre?" ventured the contestant, and several thousand smackers went down the pan. I don't like to be mean about it, but someone that dense doesn't deserve a handful of small change, let alone £8,000.

"What's the currency of Italy?" asked another quiz host, and the 14-year-old contestant just shrugged her shoulders. Worse than not knowing was the look on her face which said that she had no need to know and wouldn't be troubling herself to learn, either.

On Blockbusters, that much under-rated teenagers' quiz which deserved a primetime slot, one long drink of water was asked: "What J is a nickname given to elephants and airliners?"

"Toby," he said.

You might argue that education is a continual process, and that experience and encounter will teach young people as they grow older and will fill in the gaps.

I'm not so sure. In the Sixties, ours was an average primary-school class in an average village in an average part of Scotland, but every one of the 40 of us knew the capitals of Europe, the key dates of British history, potted biographies of 20th-century figures, the basics of musical notation and a thousand other things. We could identify species of tree and knew rudimentary botany. Most of us could parse, and all of us could tackle mental arithmetic.

These days, you're lucky to find 15-year-olds as well informed as we nine-year-olds were in the Sixties. They're filled with opinions and able to identify the latest Playstation game from a still picture, or any Top 40 band just by listening to the opening bars of the latest hit. Otherwise, they're mostly lost.

One of my colleagues found himself in a discussion about warfare and brought up the subject of General Macarthur. He was several sentences into making his point when he realised that all the younger faces looked blank. So he paused.

"You know," he said. "General Macarthur. Douglas Macarthur. 'I shall return.' "

Nothing.

"World War Two?" he said.

At which point the assembly erupted into derisory laughter. "World War Two was before we were born," cackled one. And that was the defence for being happily oblivious.

One of my aunts went to collect someone from Aberdeen Airport in the early Eighties and recalled filling in time by buying herself a cup of coffee and a piece of shortbread at the airport café.

She slid her tray along to the cash register, where a nervous-looking lassie in her late teens stood biting her lip, the open drawer of the till before her. She seemed to be looking round for someone to come to her aid.

I forget how much the coffee and biscuit cost, but let's say the coffee was 45p and the biscuit 35p.

My aunt stood patiently for half a minute, then asked the girl what was wrong. The girl explained that she couldn't take any money because the till was broken and she wasn't very good with sums. 45p plus 35p. Stumped.

A neighbour recalls visiting a bakery in a Kincardine town one Saturday morning several years ago and buying two dozen butteries for a squad of tradesmen working a her house. She took the four bags of six from the teenage part-time assistant and offered three pound notes.

The assistant rang up 9p 24 times.

In my reporting days, I used to travel the highways and by-ways of the North and North-east with various of our team of dedicated, accomplished and highly professional photographers.

One day, we had to cover a story about a young person whose parents had paid hundreds of pounds to an agency which promised recording contracts for up and coming singing stars. It was a scam, of course, and the family had been fiddled of all their cash.

The photographer framed up his picture and then said: "Now, try to look dejected."

"What's dejected?" said the lassie.

Lest you think I'm being a little hard on Scottish teenagers, I should say that this phenomenon is not limited to Caledonia. A colleague recalls his holiday of a lifetime to California and bumping into two young college students from Florida, whose parents had given them a trip to the West Coast as some sort of graduation present.

When my colleague explained that he and his chums were heading to San Francisco, one of the students looked at the other and said: "San Francisco? That's on the coast, isn't it?"

And that was a university education.

I once spent a working day with an Ulsterwoman who had emigrated to Florida to teach in a high school there. She told me over lunch that she had booked a summer holiday to Paris, and that when she had explained this to her young neighbour, the neighbour had said: "Paris? Which part of Florida is that?"

But for cataclysmic thickness, you have to turn to modelling.

On one American chatshow recently, the host, Howard Stern, jokingly asked his blonde-model guest if she would mind helping him try to dispel the myth that all models, and especially the blondes, were as thick as mince. She agreed.

"All right," he said. "Who won the Civil War?"

She thought for a moment.

"Come on, now," he said. "The Civil War. Who won it?"

Then she brightened.

"We did."

All but one of the responses to this column agreed with the sentiments expressed in it. Company recruiters were appalled by young candidates' basic spelling and numeracy errors.

When one asked a university graduate who had been Prime Minister during World War II, the grad wondered if it had been Margaret Thatcher.

44. IT'S ON THE CARDS

Or how to see the hidden message in Christmas messages

"It is impossible to write a single letter that is equally interesting and informative to several dozen people everywhere from Toronto to Tewkesbury to Turriff."

IT HAS been an epistolary week in the howe. As in households throughout the country, the first Christmas cards have been arriving and, also as in households throughout the country, Mrs Harper and I have yet to find the time to pen our own for sending.

The first cards have been an interesting mixture of religious, secular, traditional, humorous and downright obscure.

I like the obscure ones. The obscure ones are better than an evening game of Cluedo.

Who are Barry and Joyce?

Who is "Your Friend Myra"?

Who are Graham, Alice and boys?

Blowed if I know. For the first couple of Christmases after we married, I assumed these were friends on the distaff side and inquired no further. The CO always gets far more cards than I do, anyway, which says a lot about how much more approachable she is.

Then, at Christmas 1993, or thereabouts, I passed a casual comment at the breakfast table that I had never heard her speak of her good friend Myra; that Barry and Joyce appeared to be such distant memories that, like Bob Cratchit and Tiny Tim, they had been forgotten, and that her mind was never exercised by the fortunes of Graham and Alice's boys, let alone Graham and Alice.

Where were they? How were they? More important, who were they?

A quizzical look crossed her face. "I thought they were yours."

Every year since, and always among the first trickles of early-December cards, Barry and Joyce, our friend Myra, and Graham and Alice and boys have wished us a Merry Christmas and a Happy New Year.

It occurs to me that all three families must be indomitable in spirit. Not once in seven years have we reciprocated — because we can't — yet never have they taken offence, and never have they been downhearted by our repeated snubs. The cards keep coming with their warm festive wishes.

If you live next door to Barry and Joyce, or our friend Myra, or Graham and Alice and Boys, we hope you appreciate them. Hang on to them. Invite them in at Hogmanay. Feed their pets when they go away for a weekend. Offer to cut their grass sometimes. You will not find kinder-hearted neighbours. And you'll be making the CO and me feel a little easier in ourselves.

Some of you, like us, will receive cards from and send cards to people whose only acquaintance with you these days is in the exchange of the cards. The arrival of one of these always inspires in me a little pang of guilt that another 12 months have passed and that no more tangible effort has gone into renewing the friendship more personally.

Have you noticed, however, that it is always these cards which contain the most curious development of all in Christmas correspondence, the mass-market letter?

Two or three of the cards which land in our mailbox each year contain a couple of folded, typed, photocopied sheets of A4.

The only concession to targeting the audience is a scribbled . . .

Dear Alison and Norman

. . . at the start and, if you're especially favoured, a scrawled paragraph at the end which declares, more or less:

"What a rush of a year. Where does time go? Hope all's well with you two. All's fine with us. Must meet soon. Give us a call sometime. Bye."

Why do they bother?

A handwritten, friendly letter is one of the great blessings of modern existence, and I read, re-read and keep every one, however short. The writer has sweated to compose it specifically for me, so it deserves better than to be thrown away.

Equally, I struggle to read these mass-produced Christmas news-sheets all the way through, because it is impossible to write a single letter which will be equally interesting and informative to several dozen diverse people everywhere from Toronto to Tewkesbury to Turriff.

For a start, you know hardly anyone mentioned in them. You're not particularly interested that their next-door neighbour's girl has been accepted to study Phoenician architecture at Bar-Ilan; that their cat collapsed in April and is still in therapy, or that David (who's David?) was invited to discuss his teaspoon collection on Radio 5 Live.

As years pass, you develop a pseudo-acquaintance with people you have never met and, in the case of Teaspoon Dave, never want to meet.

Still, for cliffhangers, they're hard to beat. Will the architect like Israel? Does the cat have a nervous relapse? Will Dave get a teaspoon Bafta?

All this and more — in 12 months.

I can wait.

Finally, those of you who work in offices or who do business with big companies regularly will be opening many corporate Christmas cards for the next couple of weeks, and interesting trends are emerging in this market, too.

Several companies sent my colleagues and me slips of paper last year to wish us the compliments of the season and to say that they had allocated their Christmas-card budget to charity instead of going to the expense of buying block-gold cards and 120gsm envelopes. They hoped we wouldn't mind.

I can't think of anyone who would mind, apart from card manufacturers.   Certainly, there was not a dissenting voice here.

We hope they repeat the exercise this time. Charity donations are far more constructive than a corporate card which is thrown away after five weeks githerin stue.

In parallel, the Press and Journal Classified people have noticed a healthy swell of readers who prefer to send their greetings via the Press and Journal, then pass their card budget to charity, than to send out cards of their own. You know the form:

> *Bert and Elsie*
> *will not be sending*
> *Christmas cards this year,*
> *but wish all their friends*
> *and neighbours*
> *the compliments of the season*

It has been a feature of early-December classified advertising in British regional newspapers for several decades.

None, however, has the élan of a Classified notice published, I think, in 1972, which I came across during my recent protracted trawl through The Press and Journal archives.

> *Mr A. Mackie will not be sending Christmas cards this year*
> *as no one sent him any last year*

> *Barry and Joyce stopped sending cards the Christmas after this column appeared in December, 1997. We hope nothing adverse has happened to them, for they were becoming a friendly festive fixture.*
>
> *Our friend Myra, and Graham, Alice and boys glory on, though. Seriously, if you know who they are, drop me a line.*

45. ONE WOMAN AND HER DOG

Or why the closest friendships are not always human

"Mary had a capacity to endure searing sunshine, hale watter, blin drift, stinging sleet and any other extreme form of weather which the heavens cared to fling at her."

IT HAS been an anile week in the howe. You will forgive me if I can't remember the provenance of the short and sad tale I'm about to tell, but Mrs Harper either was told or read about an elderly woman somewhere in the North-east who was devoted to her only companion, her small dog.

By Easter this year, the woman had become too frail to look after herself and, with no family to care for her full-time, she was found a place in a residential home.

Alas, the home did not allow pets.

Naturally , the lady was upset. Neighbours did their best to find the dog a new owner, but with no conspicuous success. As days passed and options dwindled, it became likely that the doggie would have to be put to sleep.

And there the story ends for the moment. To the best of my knowledge, it had not been resolved when the CO heard of it just before the weekend.

I mention it not to depress you, but to explain why another devoted dog-owner sprang to my mind this week. I knew of her during my teenage years at school outwith the howe.

Mary must have been in her mid-70s then, which means probably that she has gone to a far better place by this time. It's a shame, because she was one of an increasingly rare band — a North-east character.

My fellow-pupils and I marvelled at Mary for many reasons, but principally for her capacity to endure searing sunshine, hale watter, blin drift, stinging sleet and any other extreme form of weather which the heavens cared to fling at her.

Irrespective of the elements, Mary would sail up street and down path at the same steady saunter, and always wearing the same lilac-coloured teacosy hat and gaberdine raincoat in a vivid turquoise. Sensible shoes and 30-denier hosiery completed the ensemble. In six years at the academy, I can't once recall seeing her in anything else.

I can tell you nothing of Mary's family arrangements, except that I always had the impression that she lived alone, for time seemed to lie heavily on her.

Her other distinguishing feature was that she had one constant and unfailing companion. Trudy was a Yorkshire Terrier, with a coat so immaculate that she must have had friction burns from all the brushing.

She was also badly overweight — as tubby as Mary was gaunt — testament to a devoted owner who had misunderstood the appropriate number of daily treats for a small dog.

We were never entirely sure if it was Trudy's weight and little legs which slowed Mary's walking pace, or if Mary was a naturally slow stroller on her own account and Trudy was simply obliging by not overtaking.

Anyway, it was a perfect owner-dog relationship; each depended so heavily on the other.

As for Mary, beneath that stooping, careworn and aged frame lurked a deliciously dry and young wit. I'm told that whenever any stranger in the High Street bowed to make a fuss of Trudy and asked: "What's the doggie's name?", Mary would reply: "I dinna ken. He hisna said."

The name Trudy, we discovered later, was stretching a point. Trudy was a trans-sexual Yorkshire Terrier, and you don't often come across that very often in the North-east. Certainly not in the early 70s.

We realised that one afternoon as young lads on the playing field when we spied Mary and Trudy at the far corner of the perimeter path outside the school grounds. Trudy was cocking "her" leg.

Inquiries elsewhere revealed that Trudy was actually a Rudi, but that Mary had always liked the thought of Trudy as a name and that the dog had not objected.

Both were keen sports fans. Whenever a team game was in progress on one of the five pitches, Mary would be stopped at a strategic point studying the run of play. Trudy would have hauled his front legs on to the wire netting and, tail wagging, would be panting at the players.

Mary was not shy of expressing herself if she became particularly involved in a match. I can't pretend that they were expletives, but it was uncanny to experience the lung-power behind the encouragement and exasperation which bellowed from the frail depths of that gaberdine coat.

Mary was rumoured to have been a wartime understudy for the foghorn at Girdleness.

Many a goalie was left cowering in shame after Mary let fly with her displeasure at a fumbled save. Many a striker who had battered home a long ball will never again have basked in such praise as blasted across the academy playing fields, out across the town and half-way up the A96 to Inverness.

My only one-to-one encounter with Mary came in an innovative academy community programme. Some far-sighted person in the senior management team at school had decided that the community-relations scheme should involve the whole school, not just volunteers and skivers.

Consequently, I was dispatched with four boxes of Christmas groceries, hauling a little cairtie round one of the pensioners' houses a few streets away from the school.

Imagine my surprise when the second or third house turned out to be Mary's. While Trudy made advances to my shins, I explained the purpose of my call and Mary was gracious enough to be most appreciative.

Alas, she insisted on coming outside to walk me down the path, not realising that I, in a moment of carelessness, had left the handle to my cairtie lying in the snow.

Mary tripped over it and fell flat on her face. She stayed motionless for several seconds, groaning. I hauled her upright as best as I could and escorted her back inside. Fearful all at once of Mary's high-decibel displeasure, as well as a dressing-down in the dominie's office, I stayed for long enough to ensure she was all right. Besides, it wasn't long before concerned neighbours were crowding round her and glaring at me.

With typical grace, she waved away my concern. She was slightly light-headed, she admitted, "bit it's cheaper than drink".

Mary and Trudy survived together for one more summer. At the start of my last year at the academy, I missed them and asked after both. It transpired that Trudy had broken a hip in a mischanter with a cyclist and, considering his weight and age, as well as the pain he was in, had had to be put down.

Mary never really recovered, I was told at the time. She decided not to replace Trudy with another dog.

I saw her probably not more than half a dozen times throughout my last year at school. She still wore the infamous teacosy hat and gaberdine coat, but she seemed older and slower without her chum.

Were you to have described her in one word, I think you would have picked "lost".

I know now that Mary was decanted first into one of the first sheltered-accommodation units in town, then to a home and finally to hospital where she struggled against terminal illness.

She died in the summer of 1979.

46. THE CHATTERING CLASSES

Or why you just have to laugh at gossips

———— ———— ———— ————

"The conversation went on for four or five minutes more;
a wonderfully precise character assassination in the way
that only women of a certain vintage can manage."

IT HAS been a hubristical week in the howe. Now that a decent time has passed, I can let you in on a wee secret that had me laughing quietly not so long ago.

Shortly before one of the recent spew of elections, I was approached by one political party, asking if I would like to stand on their ticket as a candidate for the council.

It was a very flattering approach, but I was amused because it betrayed a weak grasp of three things, quite apart from the fact that I doubt that votes for me would have run as far as double figures.

First, you need to be profoundly off your head to stand as a councillor. What sane person willingly puts himself up for long-term mass target practice, knowing that every word will displease someone and that the hate and distrust that result will hang about him like a bad smell long after his councillorship is over?

Who in his right mind would take on the minor problems of half the neighbourhood, knowing most that most were beyond quick solution, anyway?

An occasional junket to inspect the social-services system of Las Vegas or the beach-management policy in Bali would be poor compensation for all of that, whatever the newspapers say.

Second, were I to stand for any elected post, it wouldn't be on a political ticket. Party politics is the scourge of local government, as Moray finally decided for itself, and as the Highlands have always believed. If all the effort spent sniping across party trenches were devoted to the betterment of voters, we might pay half the Council Tax and get twice the service.

Besides, no working journalist should be a member of any political party. That's not because there is anything special about journalists, but because the first people to whine and wail about alleged media bias are other members of other political parties, and it's better not to give any of them a hook on which to hang their paranoia.

But third, and most important, who imagines that a morning-paper journalist would have the time to do the job properly?

My good friend, colleague and fellow-columnist, Alastair Bisset, now blazing licensing trails in Moray Council, certainly doesn't.

Bill Howatson, our former Farming Editor, now serving on Aberdeenshire Council, doesn't either. He gave up a good staff job to free himself enough time to go into local government.

That's not a sacrifice I would make, and the payoff is that I have to accept that time will always be the thing I don't have. It's morning, noon and night, sometimes six days a week, just keeping on top of the Press and Journal, thank you very much.

That's not always clear to others. I'm genuinely surprised when people wonder — as one very pleasant lady did at a book signing last year — how I fill my time when I'm not "putting bitties in the paper".

There's a funny impression doing the rounds about how relaxing it is to work for a morning newspaper.

I barely see Mrs Harper as it is, now that term time has begun again. She leaves for school at 7.30am and I get home on most evenings after 9.30. Five days a week, our marriage consists of one hour a night chatting over a bowl of stovies before she has to go to bed. Every other Sunday is lost to us to because of the needs of Monday's Press and Journal. I'm not complaining, but the upshot is that only precious Saturdays are our own, which is why we try to keep them to ourselves.

As a result, what passes for our social life has barely a glow of a spark left in it.

We hadn't realised the effects of this until one day just before the school term began.

Mrs Harper usually gets herself one or two new bits of plumage before the new school year begins. She has to try to keep up with the pupils. She was also shopping for a new outfit for our October holiday and happened to arrive at a frockery in Aberdeen.

It was not busy; just a middle-aged assistant and a customer who looked to be a regular. Judging by the way she sat on a stool, she was more in for a chat than to buy.

Mrs Harper riffled through the racks for a moment before the assistant crossed to ask if she could help. In conversation, Mrs Harper let slip that she came from the howe.

"Oh," said the customer perched atop her stool. "Do you know that man who writes in the Press and Journal?"

Mrs Harper wondered if it was a wee joke, but said: "Yes, in passing."

"So tell me," said the customer. "I hear him and his wife are terrible snobs."

Mrs Harper wasn't sure how to handle that bombshell, so all she said was: "Really?"

"Aye," said the customer. "They think they're airchie. Nobody sees them from one week to the next. They never join in anything."

"Well, I suppose he's maybe busy," said Mrs Harper. "I believe he works in the evenings. Sundays, as well. Travels a fair bit, too."

The customer considered this for a moment, but dismissed it. "He only writes in the paper. That's all."

Mrs Harper was finding it hard not to smile.

"He can be quite offhand when you meet him in the street," said the customer.

"Really?" said Mrs Harper. "What did he say to you?"

"Well, I haven't met him, but my sister knows someone who lives in the village and she says he can be quite offhand. Doesn't speak if he doesn't feel like it. I can't be doing with people like that."

"Och, I believe he can't see his hand in front of his face if he's not wearing his glasses," said Mrs Harper.

The conversation went on for four or five minutes more; a wonderfully precise character assassination in the way that only women of a certain vintage can manage. At last, Mrs Harper took two items to the counter.

"As for that big gate they've got," said the customer, "who are they kidding?"

"I believe they installed it because it increased the security and reduced the cost of their house insurance by forty per cent," said Mrs Harper, smiling as the shop assistant bagged up the garments.

And that was when the penny began to drop with the assistant, for she began trying furiously to change the subject, glaring at the other customer, hoping to get her to shut up.

But the customer wouldn't leave her theme, and in the few moments left she ranged from the fact that Mr Harper didn't wave to every passing driver when he was out for a walk (he can barely see the cars, never mind the drivers), to the fact that the only place he condescended to visit in the village was the bank (I wish).

Mrs Harper says now that the best moment was after she signed her cheque.

She handed it over with her most pleasant smile, noting the colour rising in the assistant's face. Then she bade the two of them good-day and left, trying hard not to laugh before she got the door shut.

Good for you ladies. You made our weekend.

━━━ ━━━ ━━━ ━━━

I was surprised by how well this one went down with readers. I imagine it was because we've all been on the receiving end at one time or another.

47. TRIPPING INTO CALAMITY

Or how to scare the living daylights out of the parents of a teenager

━━ ━━ ━━ ━━

"Keeping tabs on dozens of young people is exhausting,
especially when most want to explore 15 places at once
and have a cavalier sense of the clock."

IT HAS been a refocillatory week in the howe. Mrs Harper returned home from her Saturday trawl for comestibles and sought help bringing her booty into the house. When I ventured out to the back of the car, my eyes flashed and nostrils flared. Filling the back, from floor to ceiling, side to side, was a small mountain of chocolate biscuits, crisps, fruit and cans of fizzy drink.

My diet was over.

I scooped up as much as I could in one armful and bore my burden gladly back into the house. I was about to plant a smacker on Mrs Harper's waiting cheek when she informed me that on pain of death would I even look at those items after all had been put past.

"They're not for you," she said somewhat tartly, and I knew at once what was up.

Mrs Harper is about to undertake one of the most dangerous missions in modern Scottish secondary-school education. With several colleagues, she is laying her career on the line, risking her professional reputation and tempting fate all at once.

She has agreed to go on a three-day school trip.

I was mildly taken aback when she announced the fact shortly after New Year. After her last multi-day school trip, almost a decade ago, she had sworn that it had been absolutely, positively and most definitely the last time she would venture anywhere with five dozen teenagers.

It was not that anything particularly catastrophic had befallen them in Paris, or that an inquiry into some international incident had been launched on their return, but that keeping tabs on dozens of young people was exhausting, especially when most wanted to explore 15 different places at once; had a cavalier sense of the clock, and were convinced that they were a good deal more worldly than they really were.

There was also the possibility, dangling over chaperones 24 hours a day, that some minor incident would be trumped up into a major scandal, growing arms and legs on the teenagers' return, and that — gasp — the newspapers might get to hear.

But a teacher's greatest worry is losing someone along the way, followed closely by doing a head count and finding that you have one extra.

I won't name the school, but the "one extra" really happened. It passed into Scottish teaching folklore in the late 1980s after one Grampian school's trip to Germany fuelled a rush of hormones in a young Scot when he spied a comely German belle in the same hostel.

Five days' proximity to the object of his desires was too much for him and the two of them hatched a plan. How they proposed to smuggle her back to Scotland unnoticed, particularly on a school bus, was never made clear, but you do daft things when you're 16, I suppose.

She was discovered long before the bus left the hotel. Even some of the teachers admitted to lumps in their throats as the two gazed sadly at each other until the bus turned the corner.

There are the makings of a good weepie in there.

If ever you have an informal evening in the company of teachers, try to steer the conversation on to the subject of school trips.

They will resist at first; pretending that they don't care to conjure up demons, but after a wee white wine or three, each of them will try gleefully to top a previous story with a horror of their own, or one of the many stories which have become legend throughout teaching in the northern half of Scotland. Education is a remarkably small community.

For instance, there was the elderly bus driver who agreed to come out of retirement to take a school trip to Paris. He managed to join the Peripherique — Paris's fiendishly busy and life-threatening equivalent of the London M25 orbital motorway — but so panic-stricken was he by the torrent of aggressive Parisian traffic zooming about him that he froze.

As a result, he, his bus, five teachers and 44 pupils stayed on the Peripherique for almost a whole afternoon, circling Paris for nearly two full orbits before the teachers finally persuaded the driver, sweat lashing off him, his knuckles white with gripping the wheel, and staring straight ahead, that he had to take a chance soon or they'd be out of diesel.

There was the school trip which promised Paris-bound young Scots an afternoon at the amusement park in the Bois de Boulogne. What the organising teachers hadn't realised was that, as day wore on, the Bois de Boulogne did not just provide the homely fun of, shall we say, Butlin's or Codona's.

As dusk fell, ladies of the evening, with a somewhat free interpretation of what constituted being decently happit on a chill April night, began milling around the coaches. Never in the history of Scottish education have there been so many teenage boys' eyes out on stalks and jaws dropped at one go in one place.

Never have so many Scottish teachers physically hauled and shoved their charges up the bus steps three at a time, headfirst.

There was the somewhat portly young man from the fourth year of an Aberdeenshire school who had taken two cases to everyone else's one on a trip to Switzerland.

When curiosity finally got the better of his schoolmates and the teaching staff, he opened the second case to reveal a selection of loaves, softies, cheese slices, chocolate biscuits, fruit, a tin of rice pudding, a box of cornflakes and sundry other comestibles.

His mother, he said, was worried that foreign food wouldn't be to his liking.

There was the hot-blooded 14-year-old who claimed he was sleepwalking — three nights in a row — near the girls' dorm.

And, call it optimism, call it bravado, a 15-year-old from Inverness set off with a closely guarded holdall on a trip to Amsterdam.

When his mates urged their teacher to look in the holdall, and the teachers took the bait, the young man had to unzip the top and sheepishly revealed . . . several dozen condoms.

For all these reasons, and to say nothing of the late-night patrols to prevent visiting delegations between the boys' and girls' dorms, a teacher takes the biggest risk of her career on these sorties.

Why they do it is beyond me. Imagine a rickety rope bridge with half the knots loose, dangling over a 1,000ft drop in the High Andes, and with a gorge of thundering water below.

When teachers set off on a school trip, this is the rickety bridge they negotiate. If they cross it successfully, no one notices. If any one of several hundred knots unravels, they all plunge.

The biggest tragedy of all, of course, is that a carload of crisps, cola, chocolate, fruit and other healthy foods is tantalisingly within my reach for the next two weeks but, sadly, must remain firmly out of bounds.

The best bit after publication of this column was the number of mothers of teenagers who stopped me inside Press and Journal HQ and asked if pupils on trips were really so outrageous.

I said, truthfully, that I had merely reported the tales I had been told. At which point, one of the canteen ladies wailed and disappeared into the kitchen calling: "Nae my loonie. Nae my loonie."

48. DIG IN YOUR DRAWERS FOR KOSOVO

Or how to tidy your presses and do some good at the same time

▬ ▬ ▬ ▬

"Gym halls from Fife to Galloway have been filled with
velour curtains, dancing pumps, lamé shawls,
lampshades, travel irons and 1,000 other stue-collectors."

I T HAS been an eleemosynary week in the howe. I have been
going through my drawers and I can't say I was terribly
impressed with what I found. The story from the wardrobe
was much the same. And the press at the top of the stairs.

To begin near the beginning, Mrs Harper has returned from co-
chaperoning her school trip, full of praise for the generally
excellent behaviour of her brood, certain that they had been first-
rate ambassadors for Scotland, and mighty relieved that there had
been no international incidents.

She fell asleep propped against the wall beside the front door
after I taxied her back from school late on Friday night, but school
trips get you that way whether you're 14 or 40.

It was after she had slept for almost a full round of the clock that
she sprang her surprise. The school and the pupils had decided to
do something practical for refugees of Kosovo. They would
organise a collection of good-quality second-hand clothes for
prompt dispatch, with one or two goodie-bags to raise the spirits.

A splendid idea, I said.

By the way, have you noticed that it always seems to be schools
and teenagers who take the practical action without much fuss,
and that the people who ram their opinions down your throat (as

if opinions mattered a tuppenny toss) generally sit on their backsides, braying from the sidelines about how dreadful it all is?

Anyway, the upshot was that for most of Saturday afternoon we scoured almost every corner in the house for items that might be functional and comforting.

I say functional because, as the organisers had warned well, there is very little point in sending wedding hats, handbags, swimming trunks and the like to Kosovo. You might think that that much would be obvious, but other collections at other Scottish schools have found otherwise, it seems, and gym halls from Fife to Galloway have been filled with velour curtains, patent-leather dancing pumps, lamé shawls, lampshades, travel irons, old Instamatics and a thousand other stue-collectors.

They'll have been given with good heart and for the best intentions, and if anyone has the time they might still raise money at a jumble sale or some such, but for the moment donors need to try to imagine which items they would crave most were they homeless and on the run.

Imagine it well and you'll frighten yourself.

This is where teenagers are so adept. While the rest of us riffle through favourite working shirts, old trousers that don't fit and shoes that are being kept for sentimental reasons and little else, teenagers have the practicalities cracked.

They are the ones who put together drawstring bags of soap, toothbrush, toothpaste, shampoo, comb and razor. They are the ones spending a little of their Saturday-job money on a couple of jars of baby food, or tins of the basics, or packets of pulses, or off-the-shelf medicines such as aspirin, water-purifying tablets, cough syrups and the like.

The last time such a wave of appeals ran across Scotland, at the height of the Bosnian sieges in 1994, and the time before that, Romania in 1989, Scots had not yet come to grips with the principles of making up food parcels.

I remember talking to one of the deputy directors of a major Scottish charity that had thrown its weight behind transporting relief supplies to the Balkans and Romania. He said that he and his colleagues marvelled and despaired at the food items which Scots thought would be suitable in the Balkans, including tinned steak-and-kidney pies, puff candy, cans of mushy peas, blocks of jelly, tins of artificial spray cream and little drums of sprinkle-on salt-and-vinegar flavouring.

He said that he spent a whole morning with his colleagues sitting round a conference table wondering how to reject such gifts as tactfully and graciously as possible, on the grounds that they were barely edible in Scotland, let alone in refugee camps whose residents had been abused enough as it was.

Ultimately, he decided it was more time-efficient, and less hurtful to deeply caring people, to accept the lot, ship it out and let the charity-workers on the ground explain to the mystified recipients that Scotland was a land of broad and frequently curious culinary tastes.

Food-related blunders appear to be happening not so much this time. There's still the odd packet of lemon-flavoured fried-chicken batter powder, or jar of pour-on damson-and-apple pie topping, but on the whole we're learning.

Our weakness this time round, apparently, is toys. We see heart-rending pictures in newspapers and on television of wide-eyed, frightened and vulnerable children and our first instinct is to go up into the loft and look out a teddy-bear.

It's a perfectly natural reaction to offer a frightened child something to cling to and to hope that a teddy-bear will provide comfort.

The trouble is that so many other people have done it already. Charities are neck-deep in cuddly toys, games and story books, and don't have the resources to store or to ship them as long as other, more-practical needs have to take priority.

Indeed, so generous with toys has been the UK as a whole that some charities doubt that there are enough potential takers in the Balkans to consume this stand-by toy mountain.

This is why almost every charity operating in Balkan relief has asked the media in the UK and Ireland to ask readers and viewers to hold back on the toys and instead to consider parcelling up warm clothing, basic foodstuffs (non-perishable, obviously) and non-prescription medicines and toiletries.

Which brings me back to our own small contribution to the school's spirited effort, and why some of my favourite old jackets and breeks will be heading south-east shortly.

I'm glad to reclaim the wardrobe space, but I'm sorry to see them go. They saw me through many a press conference as a young journalist, as well as a good deal of doorstepping (I never liked it) and sleeping at council meetings.

Why I held on to them, I'm not entirely sure. Like most men, I found that they just sort of accumulated as I acquired new ones. I didn't have the heart to throw them out because, basically, there was nothing wrong with them. I'd simply grown tired of them and had felt the need for new plumage.

So they're gone.

I could pretend that I wrestled with the decision, and that sentimentality was the toughest obstacle, but I would be lying to you and kidding myself.

The reason that the decision was so easy, apart from the fact that they might do some good, is that not one item fits me any more.

I maintain that they have shrunk from being hung in the dark for so long. Mrs Harper disputes this and has another theory entirely.

Wives can be so hurtful.

——— ——— ——— ———

The surprising thing about tidying out your drawers and cupboards is that you can dispatch three huge crates of stuff and seem to create no extra storage space at all.

The other surprise is how many of your favourite clothes that you were keeping back for sentimental reasons, but which your wife never liked, are suddenly and mysteriously nowhere to be found.

49. DEATH OF A PRINCESS

Or how England went stupidly hysterical

---

*"How disgraceful that any family, royal or otherwise,
should be required to display its grief to satisfy the piety
of public and journalists."*

IT WAS the most pathetic and shaming image of the week.
Under the approving stare of reporters and camera crews, the
Royal Family affected to study floral tributes at the gates of
Balmoral Castle on Thursday evening.

And why?

The media demanded it. The media had judged that the Royal
Family was not sufficiently upset by the death of the Princess of
Wales and held that proof to the contrary was a public right. How
disgraceful that any family, royal or otherwise, should be required
to display its grief to satisfy the piety of public and journalists.

How disgraceful that any newspaper editor (Max Hastings, of
the London Evening Standard) should then declare himself
satisfied that the Queen, the Prince of Wales and Princes William
and Harry had at last done their public duty.

What duty has the public any right to expect of a 15-year-old
and a 12-year-old grieving for their mother? Such intrusiveness
demeaned those newspapers which had sought evidence of their
mourning and shamed those lank-haired gum-chewers among the
public who failed to understand or respect the privacy of grief.
Half of them looked incapable of knowing what was going on in
their own families, let alone judging someone else's.

The Royal Family has been berated in English tabloids because "you should be among your grieving people, ma'am". But that's exactly where they were. They were at Balmoral.

The conviction south of the border that only in England or, better still, London, is the Royal Family at home was typical anglocentric stupidity. The family was wise to stay on Deeside in the circumstances. No thinking person grudged them the privacy.

The core misunderstanding of this tragic week has been that the mourning and funeral of the Princess of Wales are a political event; a key to the degree to which the monarchy is in tune with the public and, thus, a legitimate forum for study and criticism.

But they are not a political event. When this week is stripped of public interest, this remains essentially a family bereavement and should be accorded the same respect and distance we would expect for one of our own.

We did not own Diana.

Almost none of us met her, and even fewer of us knew her.

Lost on the millions who labour under the illusion that she was a close friend is the irony that our impressions of her were almost exclusively media-processed.

The death of the Princess of Wales has shown the media and the public at their very best and their sanctimonious worst. We have seen and heard moving and respectful broadcast coverage, and read inspired writing in highly professional production journalism, printed within hours of the Paris accident.

We have also seen public wailing, breast-bashing and tears throughout England which were entirely inappropriate; the artificial and calculated emotion of people who like attention.

We have seen paparazzi squirming to blame all but themselves; the affected sorrow of tabloid editors who provided the market in this country for the products of paparazzi intrusiveness, and the scramble of those editors to attend the funeral "on behalf of millions of readers" — until Earl Spencer did entirely the right thing and told them they were unwelcome at any commemoration of a life they had done their damnedest to ruin.

In the national gush, too many in England have lost sight of the core truth of this week; that two boys have lost their mother.

50. MY FAVOURITE CHRISTMAS

Or how to have the best yuletide you'll ever have

▬ ▬ ▬ ▬

"Closing the entire hotel would barely have achieved the
necessary economies. Although all of us knew it, we were
all being paid, and that was enough to keep us quiet."

THEY say that everyone remembers one Christmas above all others. For me, it was Christmas 1975. I was in my late teens and had a holiday job as a porter at a renowned — if not notorious — tourist hotel in the Highlands. It was one of those huge, turn-of-the-century establishments with so many rooms that it needed at least 30% occupancy to keep it in business. I'm afraid that 30% occupancy was precisely what it did not have that Christmas of 1975. It was barely scraping 0%.

While other hotels were close enough to the Cairngorms to cream off the lucrative ski trade, we weren't. While others were close enough to Inverness to be able to promise guests a romantic log-fire Yule in the Highland Capital, we weren't that either.

So infrequent were our visitors that the owner closed down the staff accommodation block to try to save money and installed the staff in guest rooms on the top floor, but that only tinkered with the root problem. Closing the entire hotel would barely have achieved the necessary economies. Although all of us knew it, we were also all being paid, and that was enough to keep us quiet.

Chef had the most difficult job. Those were the days when coach-holiday hotels cooked meals from scratch instead of banging ready-plated frozen stuff into a microwave, adding a skite of mashed tatties and presenting it as home cooking. Cooking in such a hotel seemed to us untutored souls to be like captaining an oil-tanker. Fine-tuning to daily demand was difficult, if not impossible.

Daily, Chef had to place orders with wholesalers for produce that he might or might not need. He had to draw up menus that might or might not see tables. He had to begin cooking dishes that might or might not find stomachs.

Some of the full-time waitresses were paid off. Others were put on piecework. The ones who lived in the village were told that they would receive the call to duty as and when needed. Some of them might still be sitting beside their phones, covered in cobwebs, for all I know.

Some of my non-kitchen colleagues couldn't hack the boredom and decided that the slump was an omen pushing them to spread their wings; to explore the world; to get their names in lights and make their fortunes, so three of them took a bus to Kingussie.

By the middle of December, the summer choke of Wallace Arnold and National Express holiday coaches had dwindled to one 30-seater a week, and that carried only five Lancashire pensioners who had refused to pay £45 for 10 summer days' full-board and transport on the Caledonian Cornucopia because, by waiting until December and tholing a bit of blin drift, they could do the 12-night Winter Wonderland for £39.

You may take it that the tips were thin.

By December 20, we were down to two porters, two barmen, two waitresses, two housemaids, two receptionists, half a dozen kitchen staff and Chef.

And now no guests. Even the Lancashire pensioners were staying at their own firesides.

A porter with no cases to port occupies himself with all manner of odd jobs that otherwise never get done.

That Christmas, the village had never seen such gleaming brass on the hotel's front door. Women were checking their make-up in it. Men could have shaved in it. Brasso shares doubled on the Stock Exchange.

The housemaids were hoovering carpets to death. The

receptionists had sorted the change-drawer coins into date order. Waitresses taught themselves 117 new ways to fold napkins.

The supreme irony was that no hotel anywhere had been better ready to receive guests and deliver a first-class service. And no guests could be persuaded even to set foot on the first step up to the front door.

When the owner summoned a staff meeting on December 22 or 23 and called us round the log fire in front of reception (you've never seen logs arranged so artistically, or coal so polished), we attended with heavy hearts. We knew what was coming even before he began speaking.

Except that we didn't.

He proposed that as the register was blank and advance bookings were so thin, we should treat ourselves to lunch on Christmas Eve at his expense. He would supply the raw materials and facilities, provided that we did all the work.

I have not had a finer Christmas bonus.

City traders might have £1million thank-you cheques pushed into their hands every Christmas Eve. Chief executives might rake in an extra £400,000 in profit-related share options. Company directors might waddle to their cars carrying crates of the Macallan and half a dozen plum duffs. Oil-company employees might receive £2,000 holiday vouchers from a grateful company. Aberdeen Journals might pay my December salary into the bank three days before it is due. But I have not been more touched by a pre-Christmas gesture than I was in 1975.

You have not seen a hotel kitchen operating with so much good humour and co-operation. The usual fluorescence which hangs in a hotel kitchen's evening air, when the stress and pressure are at their zenith, was gone; replaced by banter and bonhomie.

The housemaids took special care with the dusting and hoovering in the dining room. The laundry staff pressed the tablecloth until it was razor sharp. The porters had the chairs arranged just so. The napkins have not been equalled in the history of napkin science. The food still ranks among the best that that, or any other, hotel kitchen has turned out.

You know, of course, what's coming next.

A guest arrived.

He had not booked. He had not even expected to need a room, but he was a commercial traveller who had had to stay behind a little longer than expected in Inverness to close a deal and had been hurrying home to Wrexham, as I recall, when he had broken down a few miles north of the village.

The AA was on its way, he said, but he had a feeling the problem was profound, involving his big end, and had we a room for the night?

I don't think the man had known such a welcome in his entire hotel-bound career, for he was installed in our finest room (No.52) and was invited to join the staff Christmas party, which he did with great gusto.

There is at least one Welshman who rates a Scottish Christmas as the finest anywhere in the world.

Which, of course, it is.

And while tomorrow might or might not match my yuletide of 1975 for weirdness, I hope that it — and yours — matches it for good company, good humour and good times.

From me, the CO, and Stronach the Dog, have a very merry Christmas.

The hotel has had a chequered history since the mid-1970s, passing through several hands with varying success. Its best chance of a rebirth is now.

A good thing, too, because I maintain strongly that all teenagers should have their education finished by working in such a place.

At least it gives you the resources to cope with the weirder elements thrown at you in later life.

51. AS OLD AS YOU'RE FEELING

Or why some pensioners enjoy themselves more than youngsters do

▬ ▬ ▬ ▬

"She was more entertaining than most chatter-party guests, and was possessed of a 20-year-old's humour. The combination of mischief and maturity was electric."

IT HAS been a culinary week in the howe. Hands up whoever remembers Jennifer Paterson, the saggy-eyed, gravel-voiced One Fat Lady who stole virtually every programme in which she appeared. With better jowls than Rin Tin Tin, more spluttering than a gas fire at a low peep and a form hewn from solid tweed, she was hardly forgettable. Well, I met her this week.

Not the real Jennifer Paterson, of course; she died in 1999, but a woman so uncannily similar in voice, manner and bearing that I couldn't help staring, and I'm afraid she caught my gaze and marched across to strike up a conversation.

She was more entertaining than most chatter-party guests, and was possessed of a 20-year-old's humour. The combination of mischief and maturity was electric. We'll call her Evelyn.

Evelyn has had a very trying seventh decade. Divorced from a husband of 40 years because "he was beginning to get on my nerves". Off to get a hip replacement soon after years of putting it off because she can't bear doctors "fiddling with my bits and, anyway, the dog's been promised the bone".

Raised three children — one a nurse, one something in the City, and one "an absolute waster who won't leave my apron strings. He's 38 and I'm booting the blighter out after Christmas".

Evelyn proves that pensioners know better than young people how to realise dreams: she spent part of her divorce settlement hiring a Porsche for a week.

"An absolute dream, I have to tell you. An absolute dream. I took an old friend and my golden lab out for a spin up the M1 and we drove into a service area and just sat there for a few minutes.

"We saw two policemen in a patrol car looking at us very intently and a young officer got out and came across and asked if everything was all right, and I said: 'If you were driving a Porsche wouldn't everything be all right with you, young man?'

"He had the good grace to smile and say it would, so I invited him to try the car round the car park, which he did. He said he enjoyed it. The man wasn't a fool.

"Then I looked him straight in the eye and I said: 'Now, officer, one good turn deserves another, don't you think?'

"He said that depended. So I said that I wanted him and his friend and their patrol car to stay exactly where they were for 10 minutes. And he said he didn't think that would be a problem although he wondered why, and I said:

" 'Because I want to give this thing a damned good thrashing up the motorway and I don't want you on my tail.' "

Before I was dragged off to speak to some party bore, Evelyn and I finished on the subject of children. I said I had none.

"Gosh, you're lucky. I had triplets. Believe me, triplets in the Fifties were still quite a hoo-hah. Hard work, triplets. Damned hard work. I was in that delivery room for hours. Nothing the doctor and nurses could do would persuade the blighters to show face. I was squeezing and puffing and they were doing all the mopping bit. No dignity when you give birth. Leave your modesty on the chair outside.

"I went into the labour room at twenty to five on the Friday night and I was still there at half-past three on the Saturday afternoon. Then, suddenly, like someone had flicked a switch, the three showed — pop, pop, pop — in the space of an hour.

"They brought them to me and said: 'Well done. That's been a lot of hard work, hasn't it? Would you like a drink of water?'

"I said: 'Bugger your water. I want a double gin.' "

RON KNOX (1944-1999)

"A devoted family man, a stickler for high professional standards, and possibly the most organised and prepared journalist it will ever be my privilege to meet."

THIS is the column I would never have wished to write. Today, I want to tell you about one of the finest production journalists Scotland has known. He excelled not just in one newspaper discipline, but in several. He was a good friend, wise counsel, stern critic and my professional role model.

His name was Ron Knox and he was assistant editor of The Press and Journal.

I knew Ron for 23 years, but many others have an advantage over me. I didn't know him when he was a scholar at Robert Gordon's College in Aberdeen. I didn't know him when he was The Press and Journal's chief financial correspondent at the age of 28. I didn't know him when he was made the youngest chief sub-editor on any UK daily paper.

I knew him as a devoted family man, a stickler for high professional standards, and possibly the most organised journalist it will ever be my privilege to meet. The reporter, writer, sub-editor or photographer with Ron Knox at his back in a crisis was fortunate, indeed.

It was Ron who masterminded our coverage of the four logistical nightmares that every regional daily faces: elections, Budgets, honours lists and graduation week. It was Ron Knox's precision in forward planning that ensured that so little went wrong and so much went right. So, while Ron's name might not be familiar to you, his work certainly has been. Few issues of the Press and Journal in almost the last 40 years have not benefited by the pains that Ron Knox took.

Colleagues revel in Ron's humour and willingness to tell tales against himself. His favourite came from the late 1970s, while he was chief sub, the man charged with getting the paper away cleanly and on deadline.

On a quiet news night, Ron was a boss who would free his sub-editors to go home before their time. Naturally, on crisis nights, he expected the favour to be repaid. It is notable that he never had to ask.

One very slow news night, the subs were waiting patiently for Ron to give them clearance, but Ron was busy in the caseroom where, in the days of hot-metal typesetting, the pages were assembled. It was minutes before edition deadline and Ron still coping with a complicated problem on Page One.

The older hands dispatched Andrew, a junior sub, to seek permission for an early night. Andrew found Ron at a steady simmer, pencil stub characteristically behind his right ear, shirt sleeves rolled up. He was standing beside three caseroom staff all struggling to get the page to fit.

Trying to judge his moment, Andrew hovered for a second, then said gently: "Ron, the boys were wondering . . ."

At which, Ron turned, fixed him with that piercing glare and barked: "Andrew, I'm busy! Bugger off!" Andrew retreated.

With the Page One problem over, Ron marched back to the editorial hall and found . . . nothing. The desks were bare. The coatpegs were empty. There were no subs, save a messenger tidying away a few scraps of paper and collecting the used tea mugs. Ron looked at his watch, then at the clock. "Eddie," he said. "Where the hell are my staff?"

"You sent them home."

"I did nothing of the kind."

"You did. Andrew came through from the caseroom 10 minutes ago and said: 'Ron says we can all bugger off.' "

And Ron's head tilted back and he roared with laughter.

I'll remember Ron Knox for many things. I'll remember him for when he would stick a note on my desk bearing an indecipherable scribble like bad Arabic. "What does that say?" he would ask.

I would study it and say always: "I don't know. Who wrote it?"

"I wrote it," he would say. "It's just that I can't read it."

I'll remember him for such intense devotion to his craft that whenever I borrowed a book from him I found, pencilled in the margins, dozens of corrections to the typography and the English.

I'll remember him for the time he took up smoking the pipe because he hoped it would de-stress him. He gave up three months later because there were so many calls on his time and other interruptions that he couldn't keep it lit and it was costing him a fortune in matches.

I'll remember him for his razor intellect. When Ron Knox held an internal seminar to explain how the paper would be handling something, it was quickfire stuff. Your attention had to be 300%, because the detail came like a machine-gun spray.

I'll remember him for his courteous way of handling all phone calls, even the irritating ones. The irritating ones, however, were followed by the spectacular flinging of the receiver back on to the cradle, frequently to the phone's great distress. We guessed that Aberdeen Journals' phone bill was half calls and half the cost of keeping Ron in phones.

Most of all, I'll remember Ron for the way he took an interest in the career of any trainee he thought was willing to learn. He was determined that we would become as sharp as he could make us; not just at the outset, but all the way through. He was chastising me at the start of this month for a mis-spelling committed in haste.

He spent hours in my training days, when he could ill afford the time, going over proofs and explaining why the most minute changes had been made. When someone invests that sort of time, you do your damnedest not to let them down.

I thought highly of him because he would ask me, the young loon from the country, into his office at the end of a busy day, offer me a cup of the foulest tea I have tasted, philosophise about journalism and listen to opinions. He was a great listener. It made me feel special. I had no idea that he treated almost every member of his staff that way.

I admired him because he would not accept second-best. When, one day nearly 20 years ago, I had been struggling to put together a feature that was refusing to mould, I gave up and filed something I thought would do.

He handed it back. "No," he said.

"But it's for tomorrow's paper," I said.

"I'm rescheduling the week's output to give you an extra day. You can work on it tomorrow."

"Why?"

Then came the five words that encapsulated his disappointment, reprimand and encouragement. "Because you're better than that."

They seared through me, far more than any torrent of abuse would have.

Even now, I can feel the heat in them.

"You're better than that," remains by far the most effective discipline I know.

Ron Knox died at the weekend after a sudden illness. He was only 55. Like all my colleagues, I am desperately upset.

I have seen, talked to and worked with Ron almost every day for nearly a quarter of a century and I don't mind saying that, at the moment, I feel lost.

All of us at The Press and Journal are thinking of his wife, Sheila, and his sons, David and Donald.

They might believe that all Ron's working life was contained within The Press and Journal. But we know, by the number of distressed calls from other newspapers, radio stations and TV companies throughout the country, that Ron's influence and encouragement to higher standards have gone with a multitude of P&J graduates to pervade a wider swathe of the UK media than just northern Scotland.

And when the time comes for his only grandchild, Amélie, still a wee bundle of next to nothing, to wonder about her grandfather, hundreds of us will want to tell her what a fine man he was; how much we owe him, and, to turn his own highest term of praise back on him, that he was "a first-class operator".

The Bits
at the
Back

————

THOSE ADJECTIVES

Or how one small decision can dog you for years

■■ ■■ ■■ ■■

"Like so much in my professional history, it started by complete accident. It was never my intention to have a running gag every Wednesday; it just sort of happened."

MOST of my chats with readers include two questions: are those Wednesday adjectives real words, and where do you get them? The answers are, yes, they're all real and, no, I won't tell you their provenance, because that would spoil the fun. All I'll admit is that I have to look them up, too.

How did it start? As usual, by complete accident. It was never my intention to have a running gag every Wednesday; it just sort of happened. Think of it as going one stage further than Garrison Keillor and his Lake Woebegone tales.

The most difficult part of any story, feature or column is "the intro" — the first paragraph. It has to perform three functions: it must be accurate, it must convey a striking visual image and it must lure the reader into reading further. Some of us say that half the effort in writing anything goes into the intro.

The intro on the first Wednesday column was: "It has been a wet week in the howe", which was certainly accurate, and certainly visual. Whether or not it was seductive was up to the readers.

It struck me afterwards, however, that "wet" wasn't a particularly evocative word. It didn't work very hard. So the following week, I repeated the theme with a marginally more elaborate word. Like Topsy, the idea growed week-in, week-out until I was trapped.

As far as I am aware, none of the adjectives over the last seven years has been repeated. Each one has been different. Only once have I tried to broaden my horizons and bastardise a foreign word to suit my purposes and a reader picked me up on it straight away, which says a lot for the literacy and cosmopolitan nature of readers of The Press and Journal, so I haven't repeated the felony.

The other thing I have learned is that my years at school learning the Classics were not wasted. The Latin and Greek derivations that riddle English must make spelling and definition almost impossible for anyone who hasn't canted amo, amas, amat in Friday-afternoon classrooms.

Whether or not the readers take to this running gag, I'm sometimes not sure. I've had some irritated calls from people who claimed to have looked through the biggest dictionary they could find, but without success, therefore I was certainly a liar or a chancer or both.

Usually when I probed further, I found that this alleged "biggest dictionary" was a £2.95 Pocket Oxford. I'm afraid that that won't cut the mustard, any more than a Mini will win the British Grand Prix.

My favourite story about the adjectives, however, involves the pensioners' lunch club which convenes every Wednesday. The candidate who is able to give a proven definition for that day's word has her lunch bill paid out of the kitty.

I've been thinking of putting on a grey wig and applying under a false name.

Failing that — who knows — a £5 postal order to me at:

The Press and Journal,
Lang Stracht,
Mastrick,
Aberdeen,
AB15 6DF.

. . . might work wonders.

AFTERWORD

by Mrs Harper

L ITTLE did I realise that when I married Norman that I would be marrying The Press and Journal and that almost everything I said and did would be liable to be shared with 300,000 readers. I have lost count of the times when I have been asked by colleagues, school parents and friends if such and such *really* happened; I have been subjected to leg-pulling, or asked to pass on thanks or congratulations for an item which, readers felt, had been particularly meaningful or entertaining.

Most notably, proving that young people certainly do read newspapers, I am asked tentatively by new pupils every August: "Are you the CO?" I whisper: "Yes, but keep it a secret", and off they go, chuffed to have had their suspicions confirmed.

It's that sort of reader feedback, as well as a vast weekly correspondence, that helps to keep Norman going. He has said to me often that without the spark of inspiration provided by a chatty letter from a reader, the Press and Journal might have had a large blank hole the following morning.

That's because what he does is not as easy as I suspect he makes it look to non-writers or aspiring writers. Not until non-writers or aspiring writers try producing thousands upon thousands of words a week — every week, year in, year out — and to strict deadline does reality begin to dawn. It is exceptionally demanding. There is no time for chewing idly on a pencil or gazing out of the window and daydreaming at clouds.

I have come to recognise the signs when the muse has stolen

upon him. It can happen anywhere. Suddenly, I realise I'm having a one-sided conversation. I'll look at him and he'll be studying how someone a few yards away is behaving, or listening to the rhythms of a conversation at the next table, or just staring at his feet, concentrating.

After years of marriage, I know just to withdraw and let him get on with it. He doesn't return to normal until he gets it down on paper. Unfortunately, he won't let go until it is on paper (or computer screen) exactly the way he wants it, which can mean his being up half the night and my turning up to school the following morning with eyes like doughrings. Norman promised me once that life would never be boring, but it gets so hectic sometimes that I find myself wishing that it would slow down now and again.

I like the variety in this book. There are comical pieces and considered pieces. There are poignant ones and personal ones. There are a couple of angry ones, because he gets fired up by unfairness or injustice, and he can't abide people who take themselves and their prejudices too seriously.

As one of the selection committee who read something like 1.2million words over three months, I found that the problem arose in deciding what to leave out, rather than what to include, but I think we arrived at the 52 best from more than 1,000 columns in the last 12 years.

Norman probably would disagree, because he is his own worst critic. He refused to be part of the selection committee because he dislikes reading past material. He sees flaws where the rest of us are just enjoying the imagery and the words. Worse than that, if he discovers an out-and-out mistake in anything, it is a disaster of unmitigated proportions and he is inconsolable for days.

You'll understand, then, that if only to have a quiet life, I am hoping that this book brought as much enjoyment to you as it has done to me, and was as near to perfection as we could get.

Alison Harper
The Howe
October, 1999